WHY READ THE BIBLE IN THE ORIGINAL LANGUAGES?

WHY READ THE BIBLE IN THE ORIGINAL LANGUAGES?

Takamitsu Muraoka

Peeters
Leuven – Paris – Bristol, CT
2020

A catalogue record for this book is available from the Library of Congress.

© 2020 – Peeters – Bondgenotenlaan 153 – B-3000 Leuven – Belgium

D/2020/0602/55
ISBN 978-90-429-4200-4
eISBN 978-90-429-4201-1

TABLE OF CONTENTS

FOREWORD

This is a collection of short essays which purport to show that, by reading the Bible in its original languages, namely Hebrew, Aramaic, and Greek, it can be interpreted and analysed better or differently than when it is read in this or that modern translation. This book is meant for the average reader, believer or not, not necessarily competent in any of the three languages. Since, however, I am going to present here some thoughts that occurred to me over my nearly sixty years' occupation with these languages, I would hope that advanced specialists might also find a thing or two of interest in my remarks and analysis of some biblical texts chosen to demonstrate my position.

MY CURRICULUM VITAE OF A SORT

When I was a pupil at a junior high-school in a small village in Kyushu, the southern island of Japan, math and English were my favourite subjects. I found the pace of English teaching irritatingly slow. By the end of the second semester in the first year I had got to the end of the textbook with my own bat. There was no library in the school nor in the village, no bookshop, either. There was no English course available on the radio in those days. I went to a general store where textbooks were on sale, no other books, and bought textbooks meant for higher grades. Having finished them in due course, I found at my uncle's an English textbook he had used at his pre-war high-school, and studied it with unquenchable zeal. When I moved on to a senior high-school in Ohkuchi, an hour's train journey away, it did have a decent library, in which I was overjoyed to find plenty of English books other than the textbooks. Moreover, an American Baptist missionary held an English Bible class every Sunday in the city. Taking up my English teacher's advice I started visiting it in order to improve my practical skills in spoken English. What I gained there was not only the practical knowledge of English, but also the knowledge of God. At home I learned virtually nothing of religion. My family was not atheist, but laid no particular emphasis on religious beliefs, of whatever variety. Through the missionary, the late Rev. Vernon Chandler, I got to know the God of the Bible as revealed by Jesus Christ. As a university freshman I was privileged to undergo an authentic baptism, immersion in a water reservoir in Ohkuchi. My father, whose career as a professional officer of the Imperial Japanese Army came to a miserable end with Japan's defeat in 1945, dreamed of his only and eldest son making a splendid career in his stead as a diplomat or a top public servant. He thought it very advantageous and sensible for me to study in the law school of Tokyo University. I, however, was adamant in my wish to major in English at Tokyo Kyoiku University with a view to becoming an English teacher, having as a Christian at my heart the best interests of pupils in a forlorn island somewhere off the mainland Japan.

At Tokyo Kyoiku University I came to know the late Prof. Masao Sekine, a creative Old Testament scholar already well known overseas. In the department of linguistics he was teaching Greek and Hebrew. Being very desirous of taking his courses as optional subjects, I sought an interview with him only to be told that he could not be bothered to teach complete beginners. I had no choice but to learn the basics of these ancient languages by myself. When I was ready, we read Plato's *Phaedo* and the book of Job. For my final, written assignment in the English department I chose to investigate how the Greek infinitive had been dealt with in some current English Bibles. For my MA phase I transferred to Prof. Sekine's department and wrote an MA thesis on a tiny, but multivalent Greek word, investigating its use in the New Testament, the Septuagint, which is an ancient Greek translation of the Old Testament, and comparing its use in contemporary Greek documents in the last three centuries BCE.[1] I was brave enough to run as an MA student private, tuition-free beginners' courses in Biblical Greek and Hebrew for Christian university students in Tokyo. My wife, Miss Keiko Kageyama at the time, was among the first batch of my eager students who were all majoring in diverse disciplines other than the biblical languages.[2] To me who was madly determined to proceed to the doctoral phase Prof. Sekine gently warned that I might not be able to make a living as a scholar in the biblical languages, whilst there was an option for me to return to the English department. He was testing, I suppose, to find out how firm my determination was. I adamantly put my foot down.

As a second-year Ph.D. student I applied for an Israel Government scholarship only to fail miserably. A short while later, however, I got contacted by the Israeli Embassy in Tokyo and informed that one successful candidate had decided to withdraw. They wanted to know if I was still interested. Keiko and and I had got engaged, and preparations for a wedding were under way. I sounded out with her: "Listen, we can marry any time, but an offer such as this is unlikely to come my way again any soon. Do you mind my going off?" She kindly obliged only to catch up with me in the following year for us to become one flesh in Jerusalem.[3] My intention was to study in Jerusalem two years at the longest. However, the late Prof. Chaim Rabin persuaded me to write a dissertation under his supervision at the Hebrew University of Jerusalem.

---

[1] A short article entitled "The use of ὡς in the Greek Bible" would subsequently be published overseas as my virgin scholarly publication in *Novum Testamentum* 7 (1964) 51-72.

[2] The Preface to my Greek-English lexicon of the Septuagint comprising the Pentateuch and the Twelve Prophets only concludes with a quote from Job 5.7 in the Septuagint version: 'Man is born to toil.' This one-man venture was intellectually very stimulating and exciting for sure, but it had also proved to be rather laborious and demanding. Some of my former students are continuing to read the Greek New Testament under the able guidance of Prof. Tai of Keio University. The group goes under the name of *kopos*, a Greek word meaning 'toil, hard work,' used in Job 5.7.

[3] In those days average Japanese citizens would not travel overseas unless you were a diplomat or posted by a business corporation. Hence at our wedding that took place the day after her arrival, mine was the only face that was familiar to my wife.

Having completed a piece on a question of Biblical Hebrew linguistics[4] in four years, I was conferred in 1970 the doctoral degree as the first Japanese. A few years before I had got to know a British friend as a fellow student. On returning home he obtained a position at Manchester University, and he informed me of a vacancy in his department, which he thought might interest me. This time my application was successful. It so happened that the department was chaired by the late Prof. James Barr, who happened to be one of the examiners of my doctoral dissertation.

In September 1970 we arrived, with our Jerusalem-born first child, in Manchester for my first academic appointment. Having taught Hebrew, Aramaic and some other Semitic languages nine years, I got the wind of a vacant professorship in the Middle Eastern Studies at Melbourne University, Australia. This application also went well. As I was preparing for the departure, I happened to be reading a novel by Charles Dickens, *David Copperfield*, in which one character, financially broke, goes *down under*, what did not exactly cheer me up. In Melbourne, too, I taught and researched into Hebrew and related Semitic languages. Despite its attractive proximity to Japan, I could not shake the feeling off that Australia is isolated from the rest of the world. I then heard of the Hebrew chair falling vacant at the University of Leiden founded back in 1575. I put in an application and succeeded yet again. I taught there 12 years till 2003, when I turned 65. In spite of the concern expressed by Prof. Sekine I managed to make a living as a Hebraist 33 long years, though I could not afford luxuries. Thus my Creator, who said "your physical survival does not depend on the availability of material resources, but on my will" (Mt 4.4), fed me and my family all those years. After my retirement I am also provided with two pensions enough to keep me and my wife going, one from the UK and the other from the Netherlands.

At the three overseas universities mentioned above, my sphere of responsibilities was confined to Hebrew and Semitic studies. However, my first love, Greek, never left me, and I kept working at it on the side, which resulted in a number of publications prior to my retirement. After my retirement I have no human employer in whose direction I am obliged to glance over the shoulder, so that I have been able to invest as much time as I please in Greek philology, the Septuagint in particular, having a good number of articles and books published in the meantime. Viewing a study of the biblical languages and ancient

---

[4] The title of the dissertation was "Emphasis in Biblical Hebrew," to be published later in a revised form as *Emphatic Words and Structures in Biblical Hebrew* (Magnes Press, Jerusalem, and E.J. Brill, Leiden, 1985).

translations of the Bible as a mission entrusted to me by my Creator I am still working hard at it.

In June 2017 I was flabbergasted with a totally unexpected mail from the Chief Executive Secretary of the British Academy informing me: "… you have been awarded the Burkitt Medal for Hebrew Bible studies. This award recognises your outstanding contribution to the study of Hebrew grammar and syntax, and the Septuagint." The medal named after an eminent Cambridge scholar, Francis Crawford Burkitt (1864-1935), was first awarded in 1925, and the Academy has been rewarding since then work in New Testament studies and Hebrew Bible studies in alternate years. At the ceremony held at the British Academy in London in September in that year I was in the company of eminent scholars each awarded a medal or a prize for their work in other disciplines. We were each allowed to make a speech of reception of not longer than two minutes. My speech read as follows:

> My academic career began in 1970 in Manchester as a lecturer in Semitic languages. On the evening of the second Sunday of November that year I switched on our TV, and saw BBC2 telecasting a well-known film, "The bridge on the River Kwai." That was the first time I got to know of those dark pages of my national history. About three months ago, when I received an astounding notice from the British Academy about conferring on me a Burkitt medal for this year, I cast an eye over the list of the past recipients of this medal, and I was absolutely stunned. I was sorely tempted to write a parody of a famous Charles Wesley hymn in the strain of something like: "And can it be that I should gain an interest in the Burkitt medal, a scion of a nation that caused Brits pain, pursuing many to cruel deaths? Amazing grace, that I should be deemed worthy of this honour!" I wouldn't be surprised if there are among fellows of the Academy those who lost their father, uncle or grandfather to these atrocities. This medal has fortified my determination to continue to journey along my Via dolorosa of biblical philology, not alone, but supported by my wife and children, until the day when I hear from up there, 'Muraoka, /tetélestai,/ mission complete.' Thank you so much.[5]

---

[5] A more recent film, *The Railway Man*, released in 2013, is played out against basically the same background: a 415km long railway constructed by the Japanese Army, Thai-Burma Railway, by employing some 60,000 POWs of the Allied Forces and easily more than 200,000 forced labourers from South East Asian countries under the Japanese occupation. The employment of POWs for a military project was a blatant infringement of an international agreement. Of those 60,000 plus POWs some 13,000 perished. The hymn by Wesley mentioned above is "And can it be."

Via dolorosa is Latin for 'way of sorrow,' a way along which Jesus walked from Pilate's court room to Golgotha, carrying the cross on which he would be hung. This phrase appears in the title of my book *My Via dolorosa along the trails of the Japanese Imperialism in Asia*, published in Tokyo in 2014, followed by an English version in 2016, and now as a further expanded version in Korean, tr. Bumha Kang, 2019, Seoul. The book is a record of what I have been doing since my

Going over the list of the past awardees of the medal my eyes nearly popped out. No wonder that the medal is sometimes said to be the Nobel Prize in biblical studies. Among those names I could spot a number of non-British scholars, but it struck me that I was the first Asian. It appeared to me that this award did me an extraordinary, personal honour, but it was also indicative of the international recognition of the rising level of biblical studies in Asia. I would very much like to share my honour and joy with a growing number of Asian scholars. I would also like to invite not only professional biblical scholars or students, but also the general public to ponder how the Bible, when read in its original languages, could be appreciated better or differently than read in modern translations of it.

As I have just mentioned the commendable level of biblical and related studies in Asia, let me mention a few examples.

In the seventies, when I was teaching in Manchester, I took part in an ambitious project launched by the Institute of Biblical Studies in Japan headed by the late Prof. Sekine. The project aimed at producing a briefly annotated Japanese translation of the Apocrypha and Pseudepigrapha. The translation was to be made from the oldest available version. I undertook to translate books such as Jubilees and Enoch from Classical Ethiopic. On the completion of the project I was paid royalties by a publisher in Tokyo. When I told this to a then colleague of mine, Philip Alexander, he would not believe me, saying that he would consider himself very lucky, if he could persuade a publisher to bring out his *English* translations of such books, not to speak of royalties.

In 2003, when I taught in Seoul, I ran into a young Korean who had just returned home with a Harvard Ph.D. in Sumerology. When he offered a beginners' course in Sumerian at a university in Seoul, he said, he had 25 students enrolled. I said to him: "Sumerian is offered at only a few universities in the world. Even if you counted all beginners taking Sumerian outside of Korea, they are unlikely to exceed 15."

In 2011 I taught one week's intensive introduction to Biblical Aramaic at a rural Presbyterian seminary in Myanmar. On meeting my students numbering about 15 for the first time I said: "You should be proud of yourselves. In not a few seminaries and schools of divinity in Europe and North America New Testament Greek may still be a compulsory subject, but Hebrew is fast becoming

retirement in 2003, teaching my specialisms at least five weeks every year as a volunteer at a university or theological seminary in Asian countries where people suffered enormous losses, wounds, atrocities, and degradations under the Japanese rule, occupation or military operations in the first half of the last century. Unlike in the case of Germany, this issue, more than 70 years after the end of the war, still remains largely unsettled.

an optional one. You have already completed both languages as compulsory, languages which are so vastly different from your mother tongue. Yet you are here to challenge Aramaic, and that taught by a Japanese incapable of speaking a word of Burmese." As an expression of my respect for their genuine love of the Bible I have decided to dedicate my *A Biblical Aramaic Reader with an Outline Grammar* (Leuven: Peeters, 2015) "To my friends and Bible students in Asia as a token of appreciation and respect."

Two years ago I taught the Septuagint at Asian Theological Seminary in Quezon City in the Philippines. At the first class I shared with my students and two of their teachers that I was overwhelmed by their interest in this rarified area of biblical studies as eloquently witnessed by the number of my books pertaining to the Septuagint and Biblical languages they had ordered, a total of 25 pieces. With one exception these books cost, even with the author's 30% discount generously offered by their publisher, Peeters of Leuven, more than € 42, one as much as € 73. Subsequently I would be told that a just graduated seminarian would earn, as a pastor in a rural area of the Philippines, about € 40 as the basic monthly salary. This dedication and enthusiasm is just beyond words.

INTRODUCTION

It is only natural that a text originally written in a foreign tongue can be easily read in a translation in your mother tongue. At times you have no other choice or you could read the text as translated into a modern, foreign tongue you know reasonably well.

The oldest books of the Bible were current in spoken form in the middle of the second millennium, that is, before 1,000 BCE, in an era many centuries earlier than when the oldest text preserved in English, German, or French, even earlier than Homer. The surviving earliest Chinese classics do not date beyond the middle of the second millennium BCE. By contrast, in the Near East, including Egypt, the background of the biblical books, written communication is known to have started late in the fourth millennium BCE at the latest. The oldest, preserved texts in Hebrew and Aramaic go back to the tenth and ninth century BCE respectively. Thanks to this widespread use of writing in such a remote past anyone reasonably educated today can read how the creation of the universe was understood thousands of years ago and how our remotest ancestors, Adam and Eve, came into being, lived *and* died, no longer in the form of oral tradition passed on from generation to generation. God Himself took advantage of this means of communication, inscribing the Ten Commandments on two stone tablets with His own fingers (Ex 24.12, 31.18). What is once written down can be transmitted to future generations for ever, even after the death of its author, and can be copied umpteen times over. Not only Jews and Christians, but Muslims, Buddhists, even atheists or anybody at all interested in the Bible can be grateful for the invention of writing in the Ancient Near East. The English alphabet ultimately derives from one of these ancient writing systems, namely, Phoenician. Other cultures of the world have their own writing systems, differing in the number and shape of signs or characters.

Having said this, the fact remains that the Bible was written in ancient languages. Their grammar and vocabulary are vastly different from those of many contemporary languages of the world. Even the average Israeli Jew and the average Greek are most likely to struggle with books such as Job, which could be quite demanding unlike their favourite newspaper. Some grammatical categories such as the distinction between singular and plural or the definite article, *the* in English, are quite basic to the biblical languages, but would be frustrating to students speaking Asian languages such as Chinese, Korean, or Japanese as their respective mother tongue. Speakers of Chinese and Japanese, however, can sigh a sigh of relief on discovering that the Hebrew-Aramaic alphabet has a *mere* 22 letters, and Greek just two more. They can be mastered overnight!

Those in whose mother tongue the Bible is available in more than one translation may be invited to compare them. They will find that there are discrepancies here and there. For instance, Isa 7.14 is of fundamental importance for the position of the New Testament that Jesus was born of Mary, a virgin. However, the word chosen by the prophet is translated here either with 'young woman' or 'virgin.' Of course, not every young woman is virgin. There are even old women who are virgin. The Greek word chosen by the Evangelists, which agrees with that used in the Septuagint[1] at Isa 7.14, cannot mean anything other than 'virgin,' as is evident from the well-known nativity stories (Mt 1.18-25 and Lk 1.26-38). This illustrates that, through reading the Bible in its original languages, you begin to understand what sorts of challenges they present and how ancient readers and translators of the Hebrew Bible struggled with them.

Greek may still be a compulsory subject at many theological seminaries. These days the theological curriculum keeps getting fatter: in addition to conventional, traditional subjects there are often added Introductory psychology, sociology and what not. Even to retain Greek in the curriculum could prove to be a tough decision on the part of board members. Someone like me who gets madly excited when a chance of learning yet another foreign language surfaces is a real exception. For the average seminary student biblical languages would be a real headache.

A few years ago, when I was privileged to teach Biblical Aramaic at the China Evangelical Seminary in Taipei, Taiwan, I was asked by a Korean student: "How should I answer, if an elder of my church here asks me why I should spend so many hours on Aramaic? Aren't there more urgent tasks such as preaching and ensuring that believers grow in faith?" Beside possible answers he could make, I also drew to his attention something that has little to do with grammar. As we read the Bible carefully, we notice that many of its authors were concerned not only about the message they strove to get across, but also the form in which it is to be communicated. There is a traditional form of poetry in Japanese known as *haiku*; every *haiku* poem is to consist of 17 syllabic letters which are further subdivided into three phrases consisting of 5, 7, and 5 syllables, and there must be included a word from which one can see in which of the four seasons the poem

---

[1] Readers interested in details of the way the Greek word in question, /parthénos/, is used in the Septuagint are referred to my *A Greek-English Lexicon of the Septuagint* (Peeters: Leuven, 2009), p. 535a.

is set. Note that we are not talking about 17 words. Non-Japanese must be excused for wondering whether a poem of high artistic and aesthetic value can be written with a mere 17 syllables at all.

The New Testament is largely in prose, whilst some Old Testament books, e.g. Psalms and Lamentations, are entirely in verse, and some prophetic books like Isaiah and Jeremiah have long sections in verse. Even historical narratives contain segments where one can identify epic quality. In any cultured language, poetry attaches considerable significance to form and style, and its vocabulary is to varying degrees distinct from that of prose. In the Old Testament we find a number of so-called alphabetic psalms or poems. This occurs in some psalms, every chapter of Lamentations, and Pr 31.10-31, a eulogy of model housewife. The first letter of the verses follows the sequence of the 22 letters of the Hebrew alphabet. At times two or three consecutive verses start with same letter. Ps 119 is unique; its 176 verses are neatly divided into 22 units, each of which consists of eight verses, all beginning with same letter. Let's look at a fragment of this Psalm found among Dead Sea Scrolls.

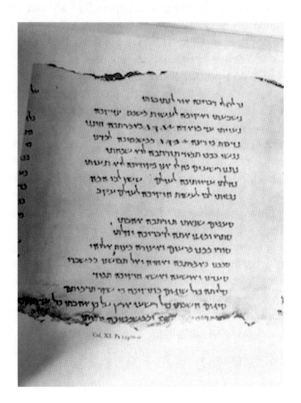

Col. XI Ps 119:10-...

We note the following details:

1) There is a space between lines 8 and 9. The division marks the start of a new letter of the alphabet.
2) The first eight lines are verses 105 to 112, and the next eight are verses 113 to 120. Hebrew is written from right to left. Each of the top eight lines begins at the far right with same letter, Nun equivalent to *N*, and the bottom eight with Samekh equivalent to *S*.

This is visually stunning. When the Psalm was recited, the audience must have been deeply impressed, hearing same consonant eight times starting at regular intervals and beginning a new sentence. Whoever wrote this psalm must have been a truly accomplished poet. His command of the Hebrew vocabulary must have been superb. One may think of a range of synonyms in English such as *good*, *nice*, *excellent*, *pretty*, *fine*, *lovely* and so on. It is not just a play on words, for within this formal limitation the poet must be able to express profound, religious truths.

In a Japanese translation of the Bible published in 1970 I was assigned the book of Judges. The song of Deborah in Chapter 5 is a grand eulogy over the stunning victory under Deborah against the Canaanites. Basically the same message is presented in prose in Chapter 4. By contrast, the song is in beautiful, archaic Hebrew. I decided to reproduce in Japanese not only the message, but also to present it in a non-prosaic form, and for that purpose I chose semi-archaic Japanese, which was still current until about a century ago. This attempt of mine went down rather well with the Japanese readership. Cakes must of course taste delicious, but their packing is not unimportant.

New Testament Greek certainly does not stand comparison with the Greek of Homer, Plato, Sophocles, and so on. Some scholars conclude that the New Testament was written in a kind of vulgar Greek which one could hear in old wives' tales or in markets. However, New Testament books the Greek of which may at first sight look somewhat primitive possess an elegance of their own, and one gets the impression that their authors are doing their very best to write respectable Greek.

When I taught at Chinese Evangelical Seminary in Taipei, I assumed that my students who must be familiar with artistic features of the classical Chinese literature would not have much difficulty in seeing what I was trying to get at in terms of form versus message. To illustrate my point I quoted a line out of a famous poem by Liu Suyu, a seventh century poet: 洛陽女児好顔色, /luoyang nü'er hao yanse/,[2] 'A lassie of Luoyang, her facial look is pretty.' The poem has

---

[2] I owe the transliteration to Dr S. Callaham of Baptist Theological Seminary of Singapore.

26 lines, each of which, as the one cited here, is written with seven Chinese characters. That same evening, one of my students mailed to me: "I got much impressed by what you taught us today. I have also written a seven-character poem, which I hope you will enjoy." His piece has four lines, and when you read them from top to bottom, you see my name to the far left, and the poem mentions my origin in the East, then my journey to the West across the ocean, a man revering God and loving people.

Last January, when I offered a week's intensive course in Biblical Aramaic at Baptist Theological Seminary in Singapore, I shared my experience in Taiwan. One female student apparently got fascinated by it, and copied the Taiwanese student's poem on the board from my computer screen. Moreover, she mailed to me the same evening, offering a seven-character poem of her own written about my wife. On the last day of the course she brought her poem beautifully framed with a gorgeous flower drawn to the right, and presented it to my wife. This time also, when you read the poem vertically, my wife's name emerges, but as the four penultimate characters.

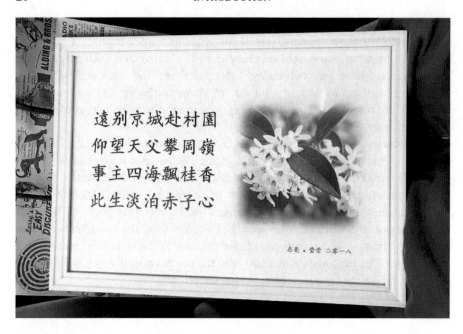

There is an Italian saying: *Traduttore traditore*, that is 'Translator is betrayer.' It means that even the best of translations can not convey 100% what the original intends to say. Reading the Bible in its original languages does not solve every problem of its interpretation. As mentioned above, by comparing multiple translations of the Bible in a given language, even when they purport to be accurately translated from the original, we note discrepancies at many a place. And yet, some aspects of the Bible, like alphabetic poems, can be truly appreciated only when you read the Bible in their original language. Any translation of the Bible is no substitute for commentaries. It is bound to reflect only one interpretation. By reading the text in its original language, however, we become aware of alternative interpretations. In the rest of this book we shall attempt to illustrate this issue by looking at concrete examples in the three original languages of the Bible. In addition we shall devote a chapter to the Septuagint as a bridge between the Old and New Testaments.

Since our book is meant for well-motivated students of the Bible, not only those enrolled in a theological seminary or a divinity school, but also any reader curious enough to explore the Bible as best as possible, the style of writing is not technical, we quote from the original text only rarely,[3] and technical footnotes are kept to a bare minimum.

Biblical texts cited in English in this book are my own translation unless indicated otherwise.

[3] When we do quote Hebrew, Aramaic or Greek, we shall avoid the use of their respective script, but transliterate instead. The transliteration is approximate, not meant to be scientifically accurate. Words and phrases in the original languages are enclosed within the brackets. A vowel pronounced at a higher pitch is indicated with /´/. Double consonants /kh/ represent a guttural sound heard in the name of the German composer, Bach. Some examples are: Greek /lógos/ 'word,' Hebrew /mélekh/ 'king.' Consonants as in English _she_ and _cats_ are pronounced as single sounds, though spelled with two letters. We are going to transliterate them with an underline, e.g. /shem/ 'Sem' and /tsiyon/ 'Zion.' /kh/ is also underlined when it is preceded or followed by another consonant with no vowel in between, e.g. /yivkhar/ 'he will choose' and /nekhba/ 'he hid himself.' The single quote /'/ inside of a word indicates a slight pause before it. E.g. /bá'a/ 'she entered,' not /báa/ with a long /a/. Likewise /qar'á/ 'she called' as distinct from /qará/ 'he called' or 'it happened.' Long Greek vowels are marked with a colon, e.g. /só:zo:/ 'I save.'

Chapter I

Hebrew

1) "She thus became pregnant for his best interests." (Gn 38.18)

The background of this story is briefly this. Judah, one of the twelve great-grand-sons of Abraham, had three sons: Er, Onan, and Shelah. The eldest married Tamar, but deceased, begetting no child. In accordance with a contemporary custom Tamar became his next brother's wife. But Onan likewise deceased with no child begotten; he had resorted to a contraceptive measure, for which God punished him. Tamar was reassured that, when Shelah got old enough, she would be wedded to him. She was not quite sure that she could trust her father-in-law. Instead, for the sake of the future of Judah's family she put on a harlot's garment and waited at a roadside for him to come along, lay with her, and became pregnant. Judah did not come for this purpose in particular, so that he did not have on him enough to pay her for the service. He promised her to send along a kid from the flock later. She insisted on getting a pledge in advance, demanding his signet, cord, and staff, and Judah obliged.

At our house-church in The Netherlands we meet twice a month for worship service. I usually take the pulpit and speak from the Old and New Testaments alternately. Some years ago I spoke from Genesis 12 onwards. Reaching Chapter 38, I started preparing a sermon and got sick of the story. I wondered aloud: Why such a dirty tale in the Bible? However, since I was speaking chapter after chapter, it was not easy to skip this chapter just like that. I make the point of making my own Japanese translation of the scripture for the week. When I closely looked at the Hebrew text of verse 18, I nearly fell out of my chair. Every one of the three Hebrew words of the text as given above in translation is quite an ordinary one. Taken by itself none of them presents any difficulty at all of interpretation. The last is a combination of a preposition /l-/ and a pronoun /o/ 'him.' This is rendered in many translations, starting with the oldest, namely the Greek version dating to the third century BCE, as 'from him.' Every beginner that has finished Lesson 5 of Biblical Hebrew would know that the combination /lo/ can never mean that. The preposition is used in the Hebrew Bible as often as 11,093 times! For the notion of 'from him' Hebrew uses a totally different preposition, /min/, which occurs 5,793 times. Words of this kind have, in every language, a great variety of senses and nuances. Even so our text cannot be made to signify that Judah fathered two babies destined to be born, which is, medically speaking, correct, but that is hardly what our author meant to say. When I realised this, my image of Tamar was radically changed.

Tamar probably had heard of God's promise to Judah's grandfather, Abraham, that his descendants would be as numerous as the stars in the sky or as the sands on the sea beach. However, she saw that Judah was most likely to die with no grandchild. She thought that she must do something about this prospect. The moment she reached that conclusion, she did not lose a single minute, acting fast. She was not getting reminiscent of the time of pleasure she had experienced in bed with her two deceased husbands nor was she after some extra spending money. The moment the 'business' was over, she threw away her flashing whore's robe, putting on her widow's garment again, never to return to the spot.

Tamar knew very well what painful consequences her most unusual action would bring about. In a couple of months every neighbour could see that she was pregnant. When the news reached her father-in-law, who was blissfully unaware that the partner of his recent one-night stand was none other than his daughter-in-law, he became furious. The woman who, betrothed to his youngest son, Shelah, dared commit such a flagrant sin, ought to be burnt to death in public, he demanded. However, on being shown the three pieces of material evidence, he had no choice but to admit that, in moral terms, he was no match for her. Villagers, however, who did not know her true motive, probably avoided her whenever she would return home to look after her father-in-law, which must have hurt her not a little.

For a woman to give birth to one baby is already a daunting physical ordeal to be endured. Even today, according to an internet site of *The Manchester Guardian*, some 16 deaths occur in the USA out of every 100,000 live births. Tamar had twins. The medical condition which she found herself in was gravely dangerous: the fact that one of the twins stuck a hand out from inside the mother's womb indicated that they were lying transversely, a condition which modern medicine, according to a Japanese midwife friend of mine, would dictate immediate caesarian section. Tamar was thus risking her physical life twice over, legal and medical. This was truly her labour of love for Judah and his family. This deed of selfless love on her part did not become lost on subsequent generations. The Bethlehemites would congratulate Boaz newly wed to Ruth: "May your house be like the house of Perez, whom Tamar bore for Judah" Ru 4.12. She also had the distinction of being mentioned, along with three other women, in the genealogy of Jesus, which is compiled according to the male line (Mt 1.3).

A few years ago, when I was asked by a local Anglican church to preach a Christmas sermon, I selected this story. Members of the church board frowned at my choice. I met them half-way, by adding a traditional nativity story and entitling my sermon "Hymn to mothers."

I, a Hebrew specialist at Leiden University, was shaken a bit, when I realised that by carefully considering one of the commonest Hebrew prepositions, a valuable truth that had escaped generations of translators and commentators emerged.

2) Abraham being tested (Gn 22.1-19)

The story told in Genesis 22 is extraordinary. This can be appreciated in translation. However, there are some interesting details which can be noted in Hebrew only.

The narrative opens with "After these things God tested Abraham." (vs. 1)

In comparison with Hebrew the word order in English is less flexible. Greek is far more flexible. A simple English sentence such as *The father bought his son a dog* has four principal constituents. Greek nouns take on an ending which shows what logical relationship is intended among the words used. In this case the sequence can be changed in Greek to *A dog the father bought his son*, in which the benefactor is still *the father*, the beneficiary is *his son*, and the benefit is *a dog*. Since the verb can be positioned in any of the four possible positions, the theoretically possible sequences number 24 [= 4 × 3 × 2]. Classical Arabic is just as flexible. Hebrew is less so, but more flexible than English. The above cited short sentence introduces a new story. The standard word order of such a sentence in Hebrew, however, would be <After these things – tested – God – Abraham>, as in, for instance, "Some time after this, the butler of the king of Egypt and his baker offended their lord" (Gn 40.1), where, in Hebrew, the verb for "offended" stands before "the butler ..." In Gn 22.1, however, the order is <God – tested>, not <tested – God>. In English "tested God Abraham" is out. I believe that here is more than a mere stylistic variation. Readers who are familiar with the standard style of narratives in Biblical Hebrew would be surprised. I would say that our author is focusing, zooming in on God.

"God said to Abraham: Take your son, your only son, whom you love, Isaac, and go off to the land of Moriah, and offer him there as a burnt offering on one of the mountains I am going to direct you to." (vs. 2)

Abraham waited tens of years before Sarah, his wife, at the age of 90, bore their first child, a son, and that happened only through God's intervention. God promised to Abraham that his descendants would be as many as the stars in the sky or the sands on the beach, and they would not only be numerous, but also many great leaders would arise out of his posterity. Abraham was long past his hundredth birthday and his teen-age son's company was his daily delight. And how could *God* make such a demand on Abraham, one might wonder aloud? Didn't His only Son teach us to pray to our heavenly Father "Lead us not into temptation" (Mt 6.13)[1]? When Abraham met a descendant of his, Paul, in heaven, he might have said: "you wrote to believers in Corinth 'No testing other than what one commonly experiences has overtaken you. Besides, God is faithful so that He would not allow you to be tested beyond what you could handle, but at the same time as testing He will also prepare a way-out so that you can bear with it [= the test]' (1Cor 10.13), what I went through at the time, I am telling you, was uncommonly harsh." The Bible records only one more example of God testing people. When God led Israelites out of the house of bondage of Egypt, they did not have a comfortable journey on the backs of camels or donkeys, but they journeyed on foot forty long years in the wilderness and were fed with plain meals day in day out. All this came over them because God wanted to ascertain that they would hold fast to His commandments (Dt 8.2). For God to put us humans to a test was such an unusual thing, and that can be seen in the unusual word order in vs. 1.

We may be sure that God Himself was aware of the harshness of the testing in both cases mentioned above. When God tested Abraham, He may have been foreseeing the suffering His Son would go through on the cross as a sacrifice for the whole of humankind.

In Engl. *the hunter killed the lion* the position of *the lion* makes it clear that the animal was the victim. Hebrew can show who the victim is by adding a short

---

[1] This is one of the standard translations of the sixth petition. However, God as tempter is an anathema, as James reminds us (Jam 1.13). Even adopting another common translation of the Greek word here, /peirasmós/, 'testing, trial,' we know James also exhorts us to be overjoyed when we are tested one way or another (Jam 1.2). I would then suggest another alternative translation: 'Help us not succumb to temptation.'

word /et/ in front of the object of the verb. In God's instruction to Abraham he was to take Isaac. However, this /et/ is found three times, not only in front of *Isaac*, but also in front of *your son* and *your only son*, where its addition in font of *your son* alone would have sufficed. Rashi, the giant among the mediaeval Jewish commentators, apparently found this threefold repetition striking, and cites a fictitious dialogue between God and the patriarch as found in an earlier Jewish exegetical document:

God	Abraham
"your son"	"I have two sons"
"your only son"	"Ishmael is also my only son born by Hagar"
"whom you love"	"I love both of them"
"Isaac"	"Why have You left me in suspension so long? You could have mentioned Isaac at the start."
"I wanted to reward you for every sign of your loyalty to me"	

Abraham did not plead with God: "Lord, please give me a grace of a few days so that I could pray and ponder the matter." He did not groan and sigh the whole night only to wake up late next day when the sun was already far advanced. He was up very early next morning, getting ready for the day's journey (vs. 3).

"Go off to the land of Moriah."

The addition of *off* is my attempt to convey a nuance of the Hebrew original here, which is compounded of the imperative "Go" and a short prepositional phrase that literally means 'to you.' This idiomatic use of the preposition indicates complete seclusion from, parting with your familiar surroundings and moving to your own world. The same idiom occurs also when God had said to Abraham, at the time still Abram: "Part with your country, your home town, and your family, and go off to the land I am going to direct you" (Gn 12.1). Tens of years earlier he had departed from Ur of the Chaldeans and reached Haran. In this half-way house he must have built up businesses and a circle of friends. To leave all this behind and head for a totally new and unfamiliar land must have been quite a challenge for him at the age of seventy-five. He would have to master a new language and get used to a whole set of new social customs. In Gn 22, physically speaking, he did not make a solitary journey to the land of Moriah, for he was accompanied by Isaac and two servants. However, from the question put by Isaac (vs. 7) it appears that he had not been told what the journey was for. The father could not bring himself to speaking to his son about it. Her son's destiny would also have been a genuine concern of his mother as well. It appears, however, that she was kept in the dark. How lonely Abraham must have felt, not being able to share the matter with anybody. Our Hebrew preposition is used in a similar way in "she sat alone away from her son about the distance of a bowshot. She thought she could not possibly gaze at Ishmael, as he slowly died" (Gn 21.16), where you could feel the painful agony of Hagar, which she could not share with anybody.

"Now it was on the third day, and Abraham raised his eyes, and saw the place far away." (vs. 4)

This verse is usually translated "On the third day Abraham raised etc.," that is, without the conjunction *and*. But the Hebrew original does have it. It seems to me that "on the third day" is in focus. So far the party had spent two nights rough on the way. Though Abraham could ponder a little at home what was about to befall him and his son, he probably needed this extra time prior to the decisive moment.

Whilst the conjunction is absent, we could interpret likewise the initial temporal phrase "in the beginning" of the very first verse of the Bible. The standard translation reads: "In the beginning God created heaven and earth." If we read this as meaning "It was at the start of God's creation of heaven and earth. He said, 'Let there be light,'" a new perspective on the creation emerges. In other words, the creation was not just God creating an empty heaven and earth, but he filled them up. The first that merited special mention as having been created with His word was light, followed by diverse celestial bodies, plants, animals, finally human beings. With the emergence of Adam and Eve the creation of heaven and earth was brought to completion.

Abraham says to the two servants he had brought along: "Stay here with the donkey. I and the lad will go yonder, worship, and come back to you" (vs. 5). Unlike English verbs, their Hebrew counterparts include, except in the present tense, personal pronouns indicating their subjects and they are indivisible, integral parts of the verbs themselves. In contrast to *I wrote, we wrote* etc. Hebrew says /katávti/, /katávnu/ etc., which share the stem /katáv-/ meaning 'wrote.' In the future tense: *I shall write, we shall write* etc. are, in Hebrew, /ekhtóv/, /nikhtóv/ etc. sharing /-khtóv/. In our verse all the three verbs, *go – worship –*

come back are, in Hebrew, in the first person plural, *we*. The first two are easy to understand, but *we will come back*? Is Abraham implying that he would come back, carrying his son's ashes in a pot? Moreover, the three verbs[2] have a special ending that shows that Abraham was not predicting and expressing his conviction of returning together with his son, but his earnest wish and desire to do so. You could say it was an expression of his faith and trust in God. He still believed in God's promise that his family line would be continued by a vast number of descendants. Earlier, even prior to the birth of Ishmael God reiterated a rosy future for Abraham. The patriarch, however, did not have even one child, let alone a grandchild. When he expressed his scepticism, God took him outdoors, telling him to look up and count the number of stars in the sky and adding that his posterity would be as numerous. The patriarch's trusting attitude met with God's approval: "he trusted the Lord and He reckoned it to him as righteousness" (Gn 15.6). The author of the Epistle to the Hebrews represents the same interpretation: "Trust is the basis for things hoped for, and a virtual proof of things still invisible … Abraham, when tested, trustfully offered Isaac, his only son … having concluded that God was capable of resuscitating someone out of death" (Heb 11.1, 17, 19). This New Testament writer could perhaps have added that, during the three days of the journey in the wilderness, Isaac was virtually dead, just as Jesus was dead in His tomb three days to be resurrected by God on the third day.

"and they two went on together." (vs. 6 and 8)

This short sentence is repeated twice with one verse intervening. The Hebrew wording is exactly identical. The brief dialogue between the father and his son in vs. 7 must have been over in less than a minute. Those of us who are familiar with the style of modern novels cannot shake the impression off that authors of biblical narratives are at times rather sparing of words. As Abram and Sarai were about to move to Egypt as short-term immigrants, he became worried that his wife, still an extraordinary beauty in her mid sixties, might put his life at a risk, and said to her: "I know full well that you're good-looking" (Gn 12.11). Among the first batch of Dead Sea Scrolls there is found an Aramaic document, the book of Genesis retold with copious expansions. Having arrived at this part of the patriarchal narrative, our Aramaic-writing author was apparently aghast at the extreme brevity of description in his Hebrew original. "Good-looking.

---

[2] As a matter of fact, the second does not, because it belongs to a group of verbs that do not allow such an ending, but parallel to the other that do have it, it is virtually there.

Is that all?" He decided to satisfy the curiosity of his contemporary readers, not just men, but also women, by playing the role of a judge at an Israel beauty contest:

> "What a splendid and beautiful shape her face has! .. how soft the hair of her head is! How attractive her eyes are! And how pleasant her nose is! .. How lovely her chest is! And how beautiful all her whiteness is! Her arms, how beautiful they are! And her hands, how perfect they are! And charming is the entire appearance of her hands. How lovely are her palms! How long and thin are all the fingers of her hands! Her feet, how beautiful they are! And how perfect her legs are! Any virgin and bride that enters the bridal chamber cannot be more beautiful than she." (1Q20 20.2-6)

The mediaeval Jewish scholar, Rashi, commenting on the above-cited short sentence writes at vs. 8 with comparable brevity: "with one mind." Before Isaac put the question to his father, the two were one pair in body only, but now they have a common understanding of their destiny. This dramatic story concludes with "they got up, and went on together, heading for Beersheva" (vs. 19). Now with Abraham's two servants, they four went on together, pondering on the extraordinary experience they shared.

A similar example of repetition occurs elsewhere, also in prose: "And David saw that his servants were whispering and David inferred that the child was dead and David said to his servants, 'Is the child dead?,' and they said, 'Yes'" (2Sm 12.19). In a common narration of a series of past events we find all over the place something like "and Lot noticed, and got up in front of them, and prostrated himself on the ground" (Gn 19.1), where the three verbs share the same subject, Lot, and it is added only to the first verb. By contrast, in 2Sam 12.19 we see *David* repeated with each of the three verbs with David as the subject. That this repetition is deliberate can be concluded from the next verse, vs. 20, which has ten verbs and nine of them have David as their subject, but it is added only to the first: "and David got up from the ground, and washed, and anointed himself, and changed clothes, and entered the house of the Lord, and prostrated himself, and entered his residence, and asked, and they served him a meal, and he ate." If this story was dramatised, a spotlight would be following David on the stage step by step. However, once the king had his anonymous prince's death confirmed, the camera started turning at its usual speed.

Repetition in a single verse occurs in a prophetic book, too: "[6]We all strayed like sheep, turning each to his own way. And the Lord brought down on him the penalty due to all of us. [7]He was pressed hard and, tortured, he would not open his mouth. Like a lamb he was taken to be slaughtered and like a sheep dumb before its shearers, and it would not open its mouth" (Is 53.6-7). In vs. 6

/kullánu/, 'we all' and 'all of us,' opens and closes the verse, stressing that we are all gone astray, and the vicarious salvation prepared by God is for the whole of humankind. In vs. 7 he who gave up his life in place of each one of us is compared to a sheep and a lamb. Neither would resist, say a protesting baa. Silent obedience is underlined as many as three times in this verse.

3) "What's your name?" (Gn 32)

In the preceding section we considered the story about Isaac, Abraham's heir, as depicted in Gn 22. Between Isaac and his darling, Rebecca, were born twins, Esau and Jacob. As often happens, the two sons differed in character from each other quite a bit. To make the matter worse, Isaac favoured Esau and Rebecca Jacob. Isaac reached a stage in his life when he began to think it sensible to make a proper arrangement over the inheritance of his possessions. If the rule mentioned in Dt 21.17 was already in force at the time, Esau would be entitled to inherit twice as much as Jacob. The time-lag in birth between the twins was unlikely to be longer than an hour. Even so, Esau had the right of primogeniture, and Jacob could not do much about it. On overhearing her husband telling Esau to hunt some decent game and serve a delicious meal to his taste so that he could make a proper arrangement for the disposition of his property, Rebecca waited for Esau to go out on a hunt. Knowing that Jacob stood no good chance against his brother, an accomplished hunter, she told her darling to get her two good kids, which she cooked to her husband's taste well-known to her. Making sure that his brother had not come home yet, Jacob took the meal to his father. His father, though not senile yet, but half-blind, having heard someone saying "Dad!," was not sure which of his twins was there. So he asked: "Who are you," to which "*I* am Esau your first-born" came back in reply (Gn 27.18-19). Isaac thought he was hearing Jacob's voice. He told the speaker to draw near to him and felt his hands. He found them hairy, and he knew that Esau was hairy and Jacob had a smooth skin. Taking note of a warning sounded by Jacob that exactly this might happen, Rebecca had covered Jacob's neck and hands with the skin of the kids he had brought to her. Thus Isaac was completely taken in and pronounced a solemn blessing on Jacob. Only a brief while later Esau turned up with a meal for his father only to realise that he had been cheated by his younger brother. He wailed bitterly and swore that, as soon as his father's mourning period was over, he would behead his brother. Dreadfully alarmed, Rebecca talked Jacob into seeking temporary refuge with Laban, her brother in Haran, until Esau calmed down. Jacob had no choice but to heed his mother's advice, and departed straightaway on a three hundred km long journey north-wards. This is a brief summary of the story told in Gn 27 and forms the back-ground of what we are going to read in Gn 32.

Contrary to his mother's estimate of a brief stay with his uncle, Jacob did not hear a word from home for twenty long years. One night, his patience having now worn out, Jacob ran away, heading home. Eventually Laban would catch up with him, lecturing him severely. However, admitting that God he served was also guiding his nephew, Laban decided to look away and let him go.

Jacob, who twenty years before ran away for his life, carrying a walking-stick only, was now on his way home with two wives, eleven sons and one daughter, two maid servants, and hundreds of cattle, sheep, goats, and camels. Though justly proud of his success and achievements, Jacob was worried over his brother, from whom he hadn't heard a word for twenty years: was he still furious? In order to appease Esau, Jacob sent ahead of him an assortment of 550 choice cattle, sheep etc. His wives, children, and servants were also sent ahead, and he remained alone at the pass of River Jabok. While he was in sound sleep, a stranger appeared, challenging him for a fight. There ensued a whole-night, fierce combat. Towards the daybreak, realising that he had little chance, the opponent begged Jacob to let him go. Jacob insisted: "only if you bless me." His opponent asked: "What's your name?," at which Jacob, not asking back "Why such an obvious question?," simply answered: "Jacob." On hearing this, the opponent blessed Jacob then and there, and renamed him Israel. Jacob got to hear what his new name implied: "I see you are repentant of your past. You have now come out a winner in your combat with God. Reconciliation with your brother is not long to come." His old name, Jacob, means in Hebrew 'to trip someone and obtain unlawful gains.' Towards the end of this very moving story we read in most translations: "and the sun rose upon him" (vs. 32). The Hebrew preposition cannot mean 'on'; the sun cannot rise below or beside him. Just as in Gn 38.18 discussed above (pp. 23-25) it means 'for him.' During the brief exchange between Jacob and his opponent the sun had already risen (vs. 27). The sun also was smiling at Jacob, as he jubi-lantly marched home in the broad daylight, having come through a dark tunnel of friction and bitter enmity with his only brother. The Hebrew verb in vs. 32 differs from the one used in vs. 27 and is better rendered with 'shone.'

Jacob named Penuel the place which would remain in his memory for the rest of his life. The Hebrew name means 'the face of God,' because, in his own words, "I have seen God face to face, but have come through alive" (vs. 31). Some time later Moses would hear from God Himself: "You cannot see My face; no human, having seen My face, can survive" (Ex 33.20). Jacob's expe-rience was truly historic. In any language we find a good number of words whose usage is highly idiomatic so that it is hard to work out how it is related to their meaning when they are used on their own. The noun *face* is one such. The word in expressions like *the child fell in the face of his father* or *he somehow managed to save his face* does not mean the flat surface of your body with a nose, eyes, and a mouth. The same holds for its Hebrew equivalent, /paním/. In the place-name chosen by Jacob it does have its literary meaning, whereas in the Bible it is used hundreds of times idiomatically. In just two chapters, Gn 32-33, the noun occurs as many as 16 times. An idiomatic translation of Gn 32.4 would be "and Jacob sent messengers to Esau his brother ahead of him," whereas literally it would be something like "Jacob sent .. before his face." Vs. 21, where the word occurs four times, could be literally translated as: ".. for he thought aloud, 'with this gift proceeding before my *face* I would like to clean his *face* (ugly through his hatred) and then I would be able to look straight at his *face*. He might lift my *face*.'" At the dramatic reunion after twenty years Esau declines to accept the luxurious gift sent by his brother in advance, Jacob responds: "No way. If you find me acceptable, you must accept my gift, please. As I look at your *face*, it looks like God's *face*. You are indeed welcoming me!" (Gn 33.10). We see what an important role the face is playing in this story.

On the day of the last judgement, as we stand, facing Jesus, we might hear Him speaking to us gently: "Don't be afraid. Lift your face. What's your name?"

4) "To increase": transitive and intransitive (Gn 35.11, 48.4)

During his stay with Laban, his uncle, he fell in love with Rachel, a daughter of Laban's, and asked her father to allow him to take her for wife. Having obtained Laban's agreement, Jacob offered to serve him for seven years. Because he was so deeply in love with Rachel, the seven years were over as if they had been seven days. He asked her father to let him be with Rachel now, and a grand wedding ceremony was laid for him. He enjoyed the first night with her. On waking up next morning, he was in for a real shock, for he found Leah, Rachel's elder sister, lying beside him. In a dark room with no light he hadn't noticed. Dashing to Laban, he protested bitterly only to be told that it was customary to let an elder daughter marry first. It may have been a convenient solution for her father to solve the problem of Leah having waited years in vain for a suitor. Laban insisted: "if you want to marry Rachel, you have to be with Leah as a married couple for a week till the wedding ceremony is over, and after that I want you to work for me another seven years." Because of his love for Rachel, Jacob decided to swallow this extraordinary demand.

Having noticed that Leah was out of favour, God saw to it that Rachel would not conceive, and Leah, instead, gave birth to four sons one after another. Her hope, however, to gain favour of her husband, came to nothing. Rachel, remembering Sarah, her grandmother, who, finding herself in a similar impasse, sent Hagar, her handmaid, into her husband's bed chamber, took recourse to the same tactic and talked Jacob into sleeping with Bilha, her handmaid, who would give birth to two sons. About the same time, Leah, who was distressed with her temporary infertility, learned a lesson from her younger sister, and Zilpah, her handmaid, produced two sons for Jacob. After that, with her sister's agreement, Leah spent a night with Jacob, giving birth to a son. Taking pity on Rachel, God saw to it that she could bear a child whom she could call her own. She herself was now pregnant, and gave birth to a boy whom she called Joseph, as she prayed "May God enable me to add (/yoséf/) to this boy." This is a frightful pregnancy race between two women bitterly jealous of each other and vying for their shared husband's favour. In some countries these days there are couples who may decide legally to marry, but are not keen on having children, and even if they decide to become parents, they desire no more than one child. Here we are in a totally different world in which it was considered highly desirable for women to marry, to become mothers, ideally at least of one boy.

The above is a brief outline of the history of Israel as recounted in Gn 28-30.

Jacob's life following his return home after twenty years turned out to be quite eventful. His favourite wife, Rachel, gave birth to another baby boy. The delivery, however, was excruciating, and after naming the boy Benoni 'a son of hardship,' she breathed her last. Jacob changed this ominous name to Benjamin 'a son of (my) right hand' (Gn 35.16-18).

Sensing that the end of his earthly life was round the corner, Jacob was visited in his sickbed by Joseph accompanied by two sons, Manasseh and Ephraim. Reminiscing of his long life, he utters his last words to the son born from his favourite wife, Rachel: "Yahweh appeared to me in Luz in Canaan and blessed me, saying 'I shall make you fruitful and multiply you'" (Gn 48.4). This encounter between Jacob and God is narrated in Gn 35, where, however, God had said: "Be fruitful and multiply" (Gn 35.11). In both passages the two verbs used are basically the same. There are interesting differences in form. At Luz God had used the imperative forms, whereas Jacob reproduced them as forms equivalent to the future tense. Moreover, in Gn 35 Jacob is the grammatical subject of the two verbs, whereas in Gn 48 God is and the verbs are in causative form, comparable with *to fell* as against *to fall* or *to set* as against *to sit*.

In Gn 48.10 we read that Jacob had begun to have trouble with his eyesight, but from the fairly long exchange between him and Joseph no sign of dementia can be detected. The incident at Luz took place shortly after his dramatic reunion with Esau, and Jacob's memory was still there. At Luz he may have thought that he was still vital enough to father more children. In the end Benjamin would become the only addition. Now looking back over his years with Leah and Rachel, he admitted with a sense of humility that it was thanks to God's intervention that he had begotten twelve sons. With his two grandchildren next to him, born to his favourite son Joseph, Jacob thought he could see God's hand at work; their mother was Asenath, a daughter of an Egyptian priest, the marriage with whom had been arranged by Pharaoh.

In the Bible we read of many a woman who could not bear a child, leading a painful life in relation to their husband and his family and deprived of the joy of motherhood: Sarah, Rebecca, Rachel, Leah, Hannah, and Elizabeth. Mary, too, who conceived a child fathered by the Holy Spirit, as well as all these ancestresses of hers, learned through their personal experience that conception was possible, ultimately, only through God's intervention.

The two Hebrew verbs translated above as *become fruitful* and *multiply* were applied to the first human couple as well (Gn 1.28). The preservation of the species was a supreme command from above.

5) Two genders (Ct 1.15-16)

The Song of Songs is unique among the books of the Bible. Apart from the question whether it can or should be read as an allegorical hymn of love between God and Israel or Jesus and the church, it can also be read as a love-song. Let's look at a couple of verses, 1.15f.:

"Behold, you are beautiful, my darling. You are beautiful. Your eyes are doves. Behold, you are beautiful, my love, also delightful. Our couch is also luxurious."

From the above translation we cannot decide whether it is a mutual adoration among the young couple or the two lines are each being said by the different partners. Beauty is not a monopoly of the fair sex; there are handsome males. Among the couple in love here *my love* and *my darling* do not tell us which partner is using which appellation. Hebrew as well as Aramaic are very gender conscious. *You* in English has four distinct forms in those languages in accordance with gender (masculine and feminine) and number (singular and plural). Likewise *your* in *I know your background* and *you* as in *I met you before*. The same holds for the third person. Not only *he* and *she* are kept apart, but there are also two distinct forms for masculine *they* and feminine *they*. Only *I* in *I am*

Jacob and *I am Rachel* is expressed with a gender-neutral form. Likewise *we, our, us*. To suggest that the mentality of English speakers is more democratic or egalitarian might be going a bit too far. I have not heard of any Israeli or Jewish feminist proposing to eradicate the feminine pronouns. These Semitic languages maintain this gender distinction with verbs and adjectives as well to a large extent.

From this grammatical feature of Hebrew (and Aramaic) we can see that verse 15 of the above quoted couplet is put in the mouth of a male and verse 16 is a response by his darling.

6) David and Bathsheba (2Sm 11-13)

From this point onwards we would like to study this well-known story and its aftermath as told in 2Sm 11-13. From time to time we shall also cast an eye on Septuagint, a Greek translation of these chapters[3] and some Hebrew fragments found among the Dead Sea Scrolls.

"With the start of a new year the time arrived for kings to go to battle, and David dispatched Joab and his subordinates with him and all of Israel, and they exterminated the sons of Ammon and besieged Rabbah, and David remained in Jerusalem." (2Sm 11.1)

The concluding short clause is preceded by three verbs, *dispatched, exterminated*, and *besieged*. Their grammatical form differs in Hebrew from that of *remained*. This has also to do with the question of word order touched upon above in connection with Gn 22.1 (p. 25). The subject *David* is up front. This is a well-known sequence when the background of a story to follow is given.

---

[3] The project of translating the Bible from Hebrew and Aramaic into Greek is believed to have started in the second half of the third century BCE. The work took more than a century, carried out by multiple translators. Once complete, it would go through a process of revision. Some such changes were quite extensive, executed under a specific translation policy, whilst others were stylistic changes or improvements. Not every book went through such a work of revision. At some stage in the history of transmission of the Greek version, the later, revised version began to be preferred, and only in modern times the original, older text form was identified in a small number of manuscripts. This applies to parts of the books of 2Sm and 4Kg, and the original version is called here 'Old Greek' or 'Old Septuagint.' In Chapter 4 below we are going to have a closer look at the Septuagint.

"All quiet on the eastern front."[4] David's army was making impressive advances. This word order highlights the remarkable fact that the commander-in-chief remained in Jerusalem far away from the war front. The story, thus, focuses on David enjoying a siesta in the capital, which would become the occasion for the affair about to be narrated, '*Love in the afternoon*.'[5]

"Now one early evening David got out of his bed and strolled on the roof-top of his palace. From the roof-top he spotted a woman bathing. She was very pretty." (vs. 2)

The Hebrew word translated as *bed* contains four consonants, the last three of which carry the basic meaning of the word, and such an identical sequence of consonants is technically known as root. Compare English <s-l-p> in *sleep, slept, sleeping, sleeper*. Twenty-two letters which constitute the Hebrew alphabet are all consonants; there are no vowel letters such as *a, i, u, e, o*. After Hebrew ceased to be a spoken language, a need was felt to ensure the accurate recitation and interpretation of the biblical and other religious texts. For this purpose a variety of dots and short lines began to be added. Otherwise, a sequence such as /l-m-d/ can be pronounced in diverse ways and bear different senses. Thus /lamád/ 'he studied,' /loméd/ 'studying,' /lmad/ 'Study' (imperative), /lmod/ 'to learn' (infinitive), /limméd/ 'he taught,' /lammed/ 'Teach' (Imperative) or 'to teach' (infinitive). Some other words such as /lmidá/ 'act of learning,' /talmíd/ 'student,' /yilmád/ 'he will study,' /limmúd/ 'education' all share the same root and are semantically affiliated. A biblical text so provided with vowel symbols is called "vocalised."

In our story told in 2Sm 11-12 the root /sh-k-b/ occurs nine times and often at crucial junctures of the story. In the above-quoted vs. 2 it is contained in a word just meaning 'bed' with no special nuance. So in vs. 9 and 13 the same word refers to a bed Uriah slept in in the guards' ward. But in vs. 4, 11, and 2Sm 12.24 the root refers to sexual intercourse between a man and a woman. In a parable told by Nathan the prophet we read of an extremely poor man who could just afford to buy a female lamb and loves it so much that it sleeps in his bed at night. The same verb is used in this beautiful, idyllic tale, too (2Sm 12.3). In 2Sm 11.4, however, David, whose lust was accidentally aroused, lay with a

[4] Alluding to a 1930 American film, "All quiet on the western front" with the First World War in the background.
[5] An allusion to a 1957 American film with Audrey Hepburn and Gary Cooper as principal stars.

woman (/wayyi<u>sh</u>káv/)[6], the wife of a loyal soldier of his who was risking his
life at the war front. Having been informed of her pregnancy, the king took
recourse to various tactics with a view to making it look as if Uriah had fathered
the baby who was on the way. So doing he committed further sins of giving a
false testimony and murdering an innocent man. On hearing of Bathsheba's
conception he lost no time in dispatching a servant to have Uriah brought back
to Jerusalem instantly. When Uriah came to report of his return, David had the
cheek to say to him: "Thanks for the trouble of a long journey. Go home, have
a pleasant time with your wife, and get over your fatigue." As a divine punishment the baby born from Bathsheba fell critically ill. On his visit to her bedroom
every night did not sleep with her in his royal bed, but lay (/<u>sh</u>akh<u>á</u>v/) on the
floor. When one looked at the Hebrew text of this story, with no vowel symbols
added, the same sequence of the three consonant letters would have struck one's
eyes. When the text was read aloud, the audience could hear the same sequence
of the three consonants nine times over.

David's lust was aroused not only because of her uncommon beauty, but also
because she was stark-naked. He wanted to know who she was, and sent a servant to find out. The servant reported: "*This* is Bathsheba, the daughter of Eliam,
the wife of Uriah the Hittite" (vs. 3). The Hebrew word order here shows a
measure of emphasis on *this*. Suppose someone is looking at a photo of three
girls, and he knows one of them is the daughter of his guest seated next to him,
and asks "Which is your daughter?". The guest might point his finger at the
girls one by one and say "This is Jane, my brother's daughter, and this is Janet,
a daughter of my uncle's, and *this* is my daughter." The position of the pronoun
for *this* would be different between the first two and the last. The king had heard
of the beauty of Uriah's wife, though he had never met her. As David noticed
her beauty from the roof-top, the couple must have been living not very far from
the city wall. Yet, Uriah refused to go home. Having got an unexpected call to
return from the front, he may have begun to suspect why, and was not disposed
to go along with his master's design. Uriah may have been aware of what David
had said that, during the war, he and his soldiers practised abstinence, and
thought that something funny was going on.

In this story Uriah is introduced as Hittite in origin. In the Ancient Near East
of the second millennium BCE there existed the mighty Hittite Empire. When
Abraham arrived in Canaan, Hittites had already settled there. By the time of
David their empire had collapsed. In our story Uriah is mentioned by name quite

---

[6] The Hebrew letters /b, k, p/ may be pronounced /v, <u>kh</u>, f/ respectively due to a phonetic rule
operating in Hebrew.

a few times. In 2Sm 11.6, 17, 21, 24, 12.9, 10 also he is consistently called 'Uriah the Hittite.' But why does his ethnic origin need to be mentioned as often as seven times? Earlier, in connection with Gn 22.6, 8 (pp. 29f.) we touched on the feature of repetition. Didn't it suffice to mention his ethnic background on his first mention? Here, too, the repetition may be deliberate. The name 'Uriah' is Hebraic, meaning 'Yahweh is my light.' It is a common Hebrew name. In the Old Testament there appear another five Uriahs. Our Uriah was most probably totally assimilated in the Israelite culture and may have been a Yahweh worshipper. Otherwise he would not have been picked up as one of thirty outstanding captains of David's army (2Sm 23.39). One doesn't know when his first forefathers settled in Canaan. Did their 'alien' origin still mean something? If he had been a genuine descendant of Abraham, would he not have been subjected to this outrageous treatment? Then it would be a case of racism.

"David sent messengers and took her, and she entered his room, and he lay with her." (vs. 4)

The expression "to enter someone('s room)" is often used as an idiomatic phrase indicating sexual intercourse between a man and a woman. Its first occurrence is in Gn 6.4. In the overwhelming majority of cases the actor is a male. Though the verb is also used in a neutral sense of 'to come, arrive,' this is unlikely to be meant here. Judah, noticing a woman at a road-side who he thought was a prostitute, would not have said to her: "Now, let me come to you" (Gn 38.16). The only instance in which we have indisputably female(s) as taking the initiative are Lot's two daughters, who, fearing that they might end up as elderly spinsters, intoxicated their father, invaded his bedroom, conceived, enjoyed motherhood, and produced descendants, a truly shocking story (Gn 19.30-38).

The Old Greek makes David the actor. This translator probably knew the idiomatic nuance of this Hebrew phrase, and may have taken pity on Bathsheba, avoiding its mechanical rendition. But there is not a single Hebrew manuscript that has David as the grammatical subject. Seeing that the king is the principal actor of the drama, he could have been presented as such, but then the verb would have to be used in its causative form, 'he made her enter his (room).' The Hebrew text as it stands may imply that we are not having to do here with a case of rape. Bathsheba may have been a consenting party, thinking that, rather than ending her life as Uriah's wife, it might not be a bad idea to be admitted into the household of the all-powerful king. If she had wished to observe the virtue of fidelity, she could have just shut the door at the royal messengers. The Old Testament knows of a number of strong-willed women who did not hesitate to order their husband round. Jezebel, the wife of King Ahab, comes to one's mind (1Kg 21.1-15). Vashti, the wife of the Persian king, Ahasuerus, rejected his command to come to the dinner party. He wanted to show off her beauty to the guests, but she may have feared that that might not be all that he was planning to do (Est 1.10-12). In fury the king stripped her of the queenship, and his courtiers, concerned about solitary nights he would spend, searched for many pretty virgins throughout the empire, seeing to it that they were beside him at night. Among those ladies-in-waiting was found Esther, whose parents had been brought by force from Israel. These maidens also "entered the king's (chamber)" (Est 2.12-15). They probably did not volunteer, but they themselves, their parents, and Mordecai, Esther's step-father, may all have seen some advantage in this arrangement.

David knew full well that King Saul, out of jealousy and inferiority complex, was after his life. When Saul offered Merab, his eldest daughter to David for a wife, he confessed how happy he was at the prospect of becoming a son-in-law of the king. But the king failed to make his offer true, but came to know that another daughter of his, Michal, was in love with his archenemy, and gave her away (1Sm 18.17-27). David may have thought that Bathsheba also was seeing an advantage in initiating a relationship with him.

"The woman became pregnant and sent a message through to David, saying 'I'm pregnant!'" (vs. 5)

One of the Dead Sea Scrolls of this book says: "Look! I'm pregnant!" One can sense a ring of her excitement. She is not blaming David, "Sir, what a messy trouble you have got me into!" We don't know how many years she and Uriah were married. She might be thinking aloud: "I've done it with one go! If not a queen, I might have a chance of becoming a concubine of the king."

"And it was the following day that David invited him" (vs. 12-13)

Most translations follow here the traditional punctuation of the Hebrew text, which has the end-of-verse symbol after "the following day." Then the author would be anticipating what follows in vs. 13. Just as the vowel symbols this end-of-verse symbol is a relatively late addition, as we can see from biblical manuscripts among the Dead Sea scrolls, in which no such symbol is used. Instances of false verse division are known. If we postulate such an accidental error here, the conjunction *and* between "the following day" and "David invited" would be highlighting the event on Uriah's second day in Jerusalem, just as the same conjunction, which might otherwise look odd and we touched on earlier with reference to Gn 22.4 (p. 28). In vs. 12 we see the king compelled to make a concession: "I will send you off tomorrow." The verb as vocalised here may bear a connotation: "I might make you go under force, if need be." David, however, may have had second thoughts. Before taking such a drastic step, a decent meal at his table might do what the gift meant to be taken home with Uriah and to be enjoyed with his wife failed to achieve, for it did not leave the city gates. If Uriah got drunk, he might do unwittingly what the king wanted him to do. However, David's tactic ended in a miserable failure again. His soldier, after a royal meal, was still in control of his mental faculties, and slept with night-guards at one of the city gates. Finding himself in a hopeless situation and absolutely desperate, David resorted to the very last course of action. He wanted Joab, his field commander, to deploy Uriah at a very perilous spot in the battlefield and abandon him there unprotected against enemy soldiers coming at him from all directions. Uriah was promptly sent back to the war zone, carrying a letter addressed to Joab. This time David's tactic worked. Among many casualties was found Uriah. When Joab sent a report to the king, he concluded with "Uriah died, too" (vs. 24). By that time Joab may have become suspicious of the king's motive for offering a temporary leave home for Uriah alone.

"and what David had done appeared evil in the eyes of Jahweh." (vs. 27)

The phrase "in the eyes of somebody" is a very common figurative expression in the Bible, and it means 'in somebody's opinion, according to his or her judgement.' Only occasionally it is used in its literal sense, e.g. "on that day the Lord exalted Joshua in the eyes of all Israel" (Josh 4.14). The Israelites who crossed the Jordan under Joshua's leadership into the promised land must have literally witnessed his impressive leadership. Later in our story we read the Lord speaking to David: "I am going to bring down on you a disaster from inside your household. I shall take your wives in your eyes and hand them to your colleagues" (2Sm 12.11); one might use a word for another body part, also figuratively: "under your nose."

What is more important at this point is that almost the same Hebrew phrase was used by David, as he instructed the reporter from the battle front to advise Joab: "Don't let this upset you" (vs. 25), literally translated — "Let this matter not be bad in your eyes." This is David's message to be conveyed to Joab, who the king feared might be rather depressed over the casualties among his soldiers. In both cases a key adjective, /ra/ 'bad,' is used. Those who read this story in Hebrew must have been shocked to realise that the king was judging what had happened in the battle field solely in terms of military tactics. The absence of the ethical, moral perspective may have been seen as lying at the core of this whole drama.

With the report of Uriah's death David may have sighed a sigh of relief now that his affair with Bathsheba was unlikely to be exposed. But God, who had appointed David as king over Israel, could not possibly look away from this history. That here lay a fatal error of judgement on the part of David is going to emerge in the next chapter.

7) Finale: Part I (2Sm 12.1-25)

"*¹And Jahweh sent Nathan to David, and he walked in and said to him. 'There were two men in a city, the one rich and the other poor. ²The rich had very many flocks and herds. ³By contrast, the poor had nothing but one little ewe lamb which he had acquired and had let survive, and it grew with him and his sons together. It would eat of his morsel, drink out of his cup, sleep in his bosom, and it became for him like a daughter.*" (2Sm 12.1-3)

The addition of the adjective 'little' must be deliberate, for every lamb is little, small by definition. It is an endearing epithet indicative of tenderness. The underlying Hebrew adjective indicates not only young age, but also small size. The lamb may have been prematurely born.

In vs. 3 there occur seven verbs in the Hebrew text.[7] The second is rendered in some translations with 'nourished' or 'raised.' Then the verb immediately following, 'grew,' would become repetitive. It is, however, often used when one lets captured enemy soldiers survive instead of beheading them on the spot or keep them as slaves, or just let go, release. This lamb may have been on sale for a special discount at the market and the poor guy could only afford to buy this. Otherwise the lamb may have been sent straight to a butcher's shop.

Later we are going to have an occasion to look at various tenses of the verb. The first three verbs in vs. 3, 'acquired, let survive, grew,' and the last 'was' are all in the aorist tense, which means that something happened in the past. The other three, however, 'eat, drink, sleep,' indicating the lamb's three important daily activities are in a tense form which indicates these activities happened in the past repeatedly, habitually. No housewife is mentioned. The man may have

---

[7] The verb 'had' here has no corresponding verb in the Hebrew original.

been a widower. We are presented here a heart-warming, idyllic scene in a humble home. Boys are mentioned, but no girl. That may have made the lamb all the dearer to the man. Uriah did not beget any child and was deeply in love with a woman who, with her uncommon beauty, had agreed to marry a man with alien background. How painful it must have been for him to lose his wife to his master when he was putting his life on the line every day in his service!

The morsel and drink, whether water or milk, could have been easily fetched from outdoors. But the pronoun *his* is repeated twice. *His* was given to it every time. His kids must have been eating there as well. So the lamb was not being fed with thrown away bits and pieces or leftovers.

"Then David became madly enraged against the man, saying to Nathan. 'As long as Jahweh is alive, the guy who did this deserves death.'" (vs. 5)

In connection with Gn 22.1 we have seen that the word order in Hebrew, and especially in Greek, is rather flexible in comparison with that in English. The Hebrew text here shows this sequence: <deserving death – the man – who did this>. By contrast, the Old Greek shows <deserving – the man – who did this – death>. The context makes it quite clear that <deserving> and <death> go together. In these biblical languages not only the initial position in a sentence, but also the final can add a measure of prominence. This Greek translator may have found it all the more tragic that the king was unwittingly pronouncing his own capital punishment.

"and he shall repay the ewe lamb four times on the ground that he did this and because he did not spare" (vs. 6)

Capital punishment does not suffice, but the guilty shall give four ewe lambs to the poor man, a very severe sentence. The noun *ewe lamb* is up front in the Hebrew sentence. The poor man is in need of substantive recompense, not just the death of the perpetrator.

Hebrew has a number of words and phrases which indicate a cause, reason or ground for a step taken. The first translated here 'on the ground that' contains a word which originally meant 'heel.' When a human or an animal walks on a sand beach, footprints are left in the sand. The figurative use of *in the wake of* points to traces left behind in the water by a sailing boat. This Hebrew expression is often used to indicate a ground for punishment or reward. Later in vs. 10 it recurs in stating a sentence brought down on David: "because you despised me."

The verb translated here as 'spare' is also used in vs. 4: "A traveller dropped in at the rich man, and he found it a pity to take one of his flock or his herd to prepare a meal for the guest who had come by, and took the ewe lamb of the poor man and cooked it for the man who had come by." This traveller probably just popped in with no previous appointment, which inconvenienced the host. It is commendable, even if you are well off, for you to make sparing use of your resources, but this rich host committed a serious error in selecting the wrong thing to spare. Around this time David had six wives (2Sm 3.2-5). Though not recorded anywhere else in the Bible, vs. 8 informs us that, on rising to the throne of Israel, he took over some of his predecessor's concubines. He should have spared Bathsheba.

"Nathan said to David: 'You are the man, for Jahweh the God of Israel said: I anointed you as king over Israel and I rescued you from the hand of Saul.'" (vs. 7)

With this sudden change of roles, we see here David the presiding judge being told by Nathan the ground for the sentence brought down by God. The Hebrew verbs for *anointed .. rescued* have an ending showing *I* as their respective, grammatical subject. And yet the Hebrew text here adds the pronoun for *I*. By means of this seemingly redundant pronoun God wants to remind David that, at two critical junctures in his life so far, God Himself was playing the main role. When David was, as a young lad, looking after his father Jesse's flock in Bethlehem, he met Samuel, who anointed him as Saul's successor. Samuel was acting on an instruction from God, who had said, "This boy is my choice. Anoint him!" (1Sm 16.1, 12-13). Till the death of Saul, his archenemy (1Sm 31.5), he would escape a few times Saul's threatening hand. On those occasions his life-long friend, Prince Jonathan and Michal, his sister and David's future wife, offered vital help at critical moments. There, too, *I* was the stage master, so God was wanting to remind David.

"Why did you despise the word of Jahweh to do what was evil in His eyes, striking Uriah the Hittite with a sword and taking his wife as a wife for yourself and killing him with a sword of the sons of Ammon?" (vs. 9)

Before this barbarity David had not been spoken to by the Lord about Uriah and his wife. The *word of Jahweh* here is meant to be an expression of God's will and thought. After having fasted forty days and nights in the wilderness of

Judaea, Jesus was approached by the devil, who tempted Him: "If you are the son of God, turn these pebbles round here into bread, and satisfy your hunger" (Mt 4.3). Quoting from the Old Testament (Dt 8.3), Jesus replied: "Man couldn't live by bread alone, but always with God's word issuing forth out of His mouth." Even if your fridge is overfull so that you can't shut its door tight, your survival does not depend on your food supply. If your Creator decides that your time is up on the planet earth, there would be nothing you could do, even if you are full of beans. Dt 8, from which Jesus quoted in responding to the devil, tells us that his distant forefathers learned this vital, existential principle in a hard way. After the successful exit from the their land of slavery, they wandered forty long years in the wilderness between Egypt and the promised land, having their novel daily meal called *manna* delivered by their heavenly Father Himself.

The word of Jahweh here relates to evils and sins we should keep away from. His will is manifest in the Ten Commandments: "you shall not covet your neighbour's wife, you shall not commit adultery, you shall not kill, you shall not bear false witness against your neighbour." David transgressed all these commandments.

Hearing "Why did you strike with a sword .. kill with a sword?," David did not protest: "I did not wield my sword." Moreover, in vs. 13 he confessed to Nathan: "I have sinned against Jahweh." As mentioned earlier (p. 34), one could slightly modify a verb, but using the same root, and give it a causative meaning. But 'causative' here does not necessarily mean force. When God fed Israelites with manna forty years, it was definitely meant as God's kind provision, though, it is true, some of them, after some time, would begin nostalgically to remember plenty of meat they used to eat in Egypt. Through Joab, his commander, David saw to it that Uriah was positioned in a most dangerous spot so that he would not return home in one piece. Just like Japanese soldiers during the Pacific War, for whom their commander's order was equivalent to an order by the Emperor, Joab would not have dared disobey David's instruction. In that sense, the responsibility for Uriah's death lay at David's door. Nor did he die an honourable death any more than thousands of kamikaze pilots who were viewed like live bomb shells. It was a fatal error of judgement on the part of the post-war Allied Occupation Forces headed by Douglas MacArthur to let their geopolitical consideration be given priority over the demand of justice and not to call Emperor Hirohito as a witness to the Far East Military Tribunal held in Tokyo shortly after Japan's defeat.

God also singled out the fact that David had Uriah be killed with a sword of Ammonites. Uriah could have been disposed of in a more "discreet" way, for instance, to have his meal poisoned at the dinner served at the palace. One could hardly think of a more despicable way of going about it than to have him killed by a sword of the enemies whom he was fighting out of a sense of loyalty to the king.

The verb translated as 'to strike' means, in a context like here, 'to deal a fatal hit,' and is virtually equal to 'to kill in the course of a battle.' Another such example is "Saul has struck his thousands, and David his ten thousands" (1Sm 21.12).

In the standard Hebrew prose, the object of a verb usually follows the latter. In vs. 9b, however, each of the three verbs occupies a second position, stressing who the victims were: *Uriah*, *his wife*, and *him*.

In vs. 9 God speaks of "Uriah the Hittite .. and his wife" as victims at the hands of David. Why wasn't she mentioned by name? Just as *Uriah the Hittite* with his background added in apposition, *Bathsheba his wife* could have been said. We have just mentioned above Uriah and his wife as victims. Is not Bathsheba viewed here as a victim? Earlier (pp. 39f.) with reference to 11.4 we wrote that this may not have been a case of rape, but Bathsheba was a consenting party. Then the true victim here would be Uriah: he was not only murdered, but also was robbed of his wife. About a millennium later, when Jesus was born as a descendant of David, his genealogy, though compiled along the mail line, mentions four women, three of whom are mentioned by name — Tamar, Rahab, Ruth — but the fourth is called "the (wife) of Uriah" (Mt 1.6). It is generally believed that the Gospel of Matthew was written for early Christians of Jewish background. Some of them may have been uncomfortable with Bathsheba explicitly mentioned in the genealogy. Was it meant as a genealogy of One who did not feel ashamed of having among His foremothers(?) Tamar, a woman who tempted her father-in-law into bed, Rahab, an alien manageress of a geisha-house in Jericho, Ruth a foreigner, and Solomon's mother whose name remains best unmentioned, One who came to save not only Jews including the author, who unashamedly calls himself 'publican' (Mt 10.3), and respectable coreligionists, but also foreign sinners?

Here is something important that need be borne in mind as one reads the Bible. What *is* written there is of course of vital importance. And what we must know would be found there. But there are matters which one might expect to find there, but are not there. It should be alright in such cases to ask why? One may be able to work out an answer from the context. Otherwise it should be acceptable to try to read between the lines and make the best of one's creative imagination, as long as we do not run away with it.

"And now a sword will not depart from your household for ever because you despised Me and took the wife of Uriah to become a wife of yours." (vs. 10)

How this frightening prediction would unfold itself can be read in the following chapters: the death of Amnon, a son of David's (Chapter 13), the death of another beloved son of his, Absalom (Chapter 18), that of Adonijah, the fourth son of David (1Kg Chapter 2), all dying a cruel death as a consequence of some or other internal conflict in the royal house. It is shocking in the light of what we noted earlier with reference to 2Sm 11.27. When David sent back a herald from the frontline, the king told him to say to Joab that the commander should not be too worried over some casualties suffered in case Joab became unduly depressive, for in a war situation "the sword is bound to devour this (soldier), then that (soldier)" as if he were predicting what would befall himself in the not too distant future.

"¹¹Thus said Jahweh: 'Behold, I am bringing down on you a horrible situation within your household. I shall take off your wives in your presence and give them to your colleague, and he will sleep with your wives in the sight of this sun.¹² You acted secretively, but I shall do this in the sight of all Israel and in the sight of this sun." (vs. 11-12)

The use of the demonstrative pronoun *this* in *this sun*, and not *that*, is striking. The form selected seems to indicate that the sun was felt to be mentally near. It would be extravagant to suggest that it was physically near to God in heaven. Conveying this message, Nathan may have been pointing his finger upwards. When David lay with Bathsheba, the room may have been locked and faintly lighted. By contrast, what is going to happen to David will take place in the broad daylight in public view.

Here, too, we note the use of the seemingly redundant personal pronouns, *I* and *you*; see above at p. 44. Clearly a contrast is intended: *you* acted secretively, but what *I* am going to do is to be in full view of everybody.

"David said to Nathan: 'I have sinned against Jahweh,' whereupon Nathan said to David: 'As for Jahweh, He has written off the penalty which is due to your sin, so that you will be spared capital punishment.'" (vs. 13)

Those directly affected by David's sinful deeds were Uriah and Bathsheba. However, he does not confess "I have sinned to Uriah and Bathsheba," but "I have sinned against Jahweh." In the preceding chapter we read that David's deeds were evil in the eyes of Jahweh (11.27), and that was also our author's perspective. In this chapter the same judgement is put in God's own mouth (vs. 9). If we look at David's deeds from the horizontal, interpersonal perspective alone, then they were directed at Uriah and Bathsheba. We pointed out above which of the Ten Commandments David's deeds constitute an infringement of. These commandments were not a product of Moses' meditation or written up by ancient Israelites. They were conveyed to Moses directly by God Himself. Some seem to think that the first four commandments are about our relationship with God and the remaining six concern our relationship with fellow humans. However, everybody was created in God's image. Hence any evil done to any human is ultimately a sin against God.

In some translations the second half of vs. 13 reads "the Lord also ..,' which is misleading, whilst others have nothing for /gam/, a short, high-frequency word in the Hebrew text. What is meant is "the Lord on His part .." Despite its shortness, it is wrong to ignore it; it shows how God is responding to the king's expression of remorse.

The sentence that immediately follows is also difficult of interpretation. Some translations read: ".. has forgiven your sin," which cannot be right. Otherwise the baby on the way would have survived. On the contrary, vs. 14 states exactly the opposite. Another common translation "put away your sin" is no less problematic. For the notion as expressed, for instance, in "the removal of his sin" (Is 27.9) and "Remove violence and plundering, and execute judgement and justice" (Ezk 45.9) a different verb is used. Nathan's message seems to be: "Strictly speaking you deserve instant death, as you yourself have condemned the rich man, but God is generously allowing you to stay on the throne for a while yet." The noun often translated here as "sin" can also mean a penalty or punishment for a sin committed. At 2Sm 24.10, David, by using the same verb used by Nathan here, pleads with God: "Please, do not act on the penalty for Your servant's iniquity."

"Furthermore, mind you, in this matter you have really despised the word of Jahweh. Also the child born to you shall be caused to die." (vs. 14)

With the translation "the word of Jahweh" I have adopted the reading as found in a fragmentary Dead Sea Scroll. The traditional Hebrew text reads "the enemies of Jahweh," which does not make sense. At the end of vs. 13 we read that the king is going to be spared death, but the same verb is used in the positive form at the end of this verse and the baby is to die. Moreover, the formulation in vs. 14 implies that the baby's death is not going to be a natural one, but signifies a death as punishment. The same wording is found in the warning given to Adam and Eve as to what was to follow, should they disobey God's command not to eat of the fruit of the forbidden tree. This is not about still birth. Nor is it about the certainty of death as implied in some translations with their "surely" or "certainly." After Adam and Even's death as a punishment by God, eventual death is an absolute certainty for every mortal creature. The baby would die seven days old. He did not live long enough to be circumcised on the eighth day and be given a name. So he would die as an anonymous prince. How sad for this innocent baby! He died the death his father deserved. His death must have been extremely painful, to his mother in particular with her first child, whom she dreamed of becoming a prince. This was a punishment suffered by the parents. This early death of the baby meant instant death of their dream. That is why we have translated "be caused to die," though the Hebrew verb here is not causative in form.[8] The Hebrew word translated above as "also" hints at this pain shared by all the three concerned.

The word translated above as "born" can also mean "about to be born," as in "Every son that is born to Hebrews you shall cast into the Nile" (Ex 1.22). But at the end of the preceding chapter we read "and she gave birth to him a son" (2Sm 11.27). At this news Nathan must have hastened to seek an audience with the king.

It might be thought that *the child born* suffices. By adding *to you* the prophet may be reminding the king once again that he had resorted to falsifying the undeniable fact that he had fathered the baby and to murdering the innocent soldier.

"And Nathan went home, and Jahweh struck the child the wife of Uriah had born to David, and it became critically ill." (vs. 15)

At the time of delivery of the baby Bathsheba had formally become a wife of David's (2Sm 11.27), but when she became pregnant, she was still Uriah's wife. This highlights yet again the sinful nature of the whole event.

The verb translated with "to become critically ill" is rather infrequent. The Old Greek translates it with "it became weak and stayed so."

"And David pleaded with Jahweh on behalf of the infant, and David determinedly fasted, and he would come in, lie on the ground, and spend the night." (vs. 16)

The king must have prayed repeatedly. Every time a servant brought in his meal, he firmly refused to touch it. When his daily duties were finished in the palace,

[8] One manuscript from among the Dead Sea Scrolls does use here a causative form in the passive voice.

he would come into the room where the baby lay in Bathsheba's arms, he would not return to the luxurious bed, in which he had slept with her, but sleep on the floor night after night. Both the Greek translation and a Dead Sea fragment add that he lay on the ground in a sack, in a plastic bag, you might say. One could sense the pathos that floated in the room. The last three verbs, "come in .. lie .. spend the night" are written in a form that indicates repetition.

"His senior courtiers stood next to him, trying to raise him from the ground, but he refused and did not dine in their company." (vs. 17)

He would normally eat in the royal dining room. Sensing that he was unlikely to do so, his courtiers brought his meal to the room where Bathsheba was with the infant. The king probably did not wish his courtiers to witness his agitation, as he ate with his hands shaking. No doctor was called in, probably because David, because of his guilt feeling, did not want the critical state of the kid to become public knowledge.

"On the seventh day the child died. But David's servants would not dare tell him that the child had died, for they said among themselves: 'when the child was still alive, we spoke to him, but he had no ear for what we had to say. How could we then tell him, "the child has died"? He might commit harakiri.'" (vs. 18)

In the Hebrew Bible we often read of so and so having lived so many years. In most cases it is about heroes who died in good old age as in "These are the days of Abraham's life, a hundred and seventy-five years" (Gn 25.7), and it records such people's end of life. In the case of this infant its life had just begun. The way the verse is introduced is a very familiar way of indicating a new turn in a story being told as in Gn 22.1 'and now it happened after these things,' but by its nature it is always positioned at the start of the story, not at its end as here.

Buddhists have a ceremony conducted on the seventh day after the decease of one's family member. Jews observe a ritual called *shiv'a*, 'seven': for seven days they mourn the deceased, sitting at home and receiving mourners. The child had lived as many days as the length of his mourning. He died anonymous. I have never seen a tombstone with no name of the deceased engraved on it.

"harakiri" translates a word which, translated literally, means 'evil thing, evil deed.' The Septuagint translated it with 'he might do evil things.' An almost identical Greek expression is used in the New Testament, Acts 16.28. When the apostle Paul and a colleague of his, Silas, were imprisoned in Philippi, Greece, there occurred one night an earthquake, and the lock of their room came off. Paul advised the prison guard not resort to a rash action, for the apostle feared that the guard, with his sword already drawn, might consider himself responsible, should his charges escape. In some culture like mine, parents committing suicide and taking their own child or children with them are sometimes viewed in a positive light for not leaving their kids as orphans and a burden on their relatives. In the biblical world, suicide is never justified. However hard to bear and keep on, it is ultimately a gift from God, even if it is your own.

"And David saw his courtiers whispering and David inferred that the child was dead and David said to his courtiers, 'Is the child dead?,' and they said, 'Yes.'" (vs. 19)

In this verse there are three verbs, all with David as their grammatical subject, and *David* is repeated with each of them. How this tenacious repetition can be analysed has been touched upon earlier (p. 30).

The noun rendered here with "courtier" is a very common word, occurring more than 700 times and often rendered with "servant." Its range of referents is quite broad; it can refer to a slave, a domestic servant, and so on. Here it must be referring to people of higher status. It is also used with reference to high-ranking officers of Pharaoh whose mysterious dreams Joseph solved (Gn 40.20). It is also frequently used as a self-effacing substitute for a personal pronoun: instead of *I, me* Hebrew also uses 'your servant,' e.g. Gn 18.3 or instead of *we, us* 'your servants,' e.g. Gn 42.11 immediately after *we*. The reverse relationship is expressed with 'my lord' instead of *you*, e.g. Gn 18.12 (wife to husband), Nu 12.11 (Moses to God).

The answer given by the courtiers is, literally translated, "Dead." It is remarkable that Biblical Hebrew lacks a word for *Yes*, which one might say is an essential component of the vocabulary of any language. Its opposite, one for *No*, does exist. Is it typical of Ancient Israelites who were dubbed 'a stiff-necked people' (Ex 32.9 and five more times)? When one answered in the affirmative, one repeated the essential word contained in the question as in our example here. When Rebecca was asked by her brother, "Will you go with this gentleman?," her *Yes* was expressed as "I will go" (Gn 24.58).

"And David got up from the ground, bathed, anointed himself, changed his clothes, entered the house of Jahweh, prostrated himself,

entered his residence, requested, and they served him a meal, and he ate." (vs. 20)

In contrast to the preceding verse we have here nine verbs, all with David as their subject, but *David* is added only to the first. This remarkable phenomenon was dealt with earlier (p. 30).

The Hebrew word for "prostrated himself" is often translated with "worship." It means going down on one's knees, to prostrate oneself with one's face touching the ground.

    The noun translated as "meal" basically denotes bread. However, the following exchange with his courtiers suggests that David was no longer fasting, so that there was more on the table.

"21And his courtiers said to him, 'What is this thing you have done? When the child was still alive, you fasted and wept, but when the child died, you got up and had a meal.' 22And he said, 'When the child was still alive, I fasted and wept, for I thought, "Who knows? Jahweh may take pity on me and the child may recover." 23But now that he has died, why should I fast? Can I cause him to come back again? It is I that am going to him, but he will not come back to me.'" (vs. 21-23).

Vs. 21 begins with "and his courtiers said" and vs. 22 with "And he said." This is typical of the biblical languages and ancient languages in general; when direct speech is quoted as here, it was the general rule to state who said to whom. This was essential for accurate communication, when there were no punctuation marks such as quotation marks, commas, periods and so on. Moreover, some languages such as Korean and Japanese know a fairly elaborate system of honorific, courteous speech. For instance, *Are you coming?* would be expressed in Japanese quite differently depending on whether a teacher is asking a student of his or the other way round. To keep repeating *he said to me* and *I said to him* etc. runs the risk of sounding a bit boring and tiresome, particularly in written translation. At the risk of going against the policy of 'faithful to the original' we should perhaps consider abandoning this mechanical approach. All the same, we may need to remember that the Scriptures are not only read visually, but also recited in public.

    For our 'recover' (vs. 22) most translators offer 'live' as a verb. Though the child's heart was still beating, he was virtually dead. The word is indeed used of someone who was literally dead regaining life. A dead man's corpse was cast into Elisha's grave, but the moment the corpse touched the prophet's bones, the man revived (2Kg 13.21). On the other hand, ancient Israelites who were bitten by poisonous snakes in the wilderness recovered when they looked up at a bronze snake made by Moses and hanging from a pole (Nu 21.8-9). If they had been already dead, they couldn't have looked up; they must have been writhing in excruciating pain. The same verb as used in vs. 23 and in the same form is rendered in the Septuagint: "they were now full of life." It would have been the king's last wish to see the infant just being artificially kept alive like a vegetable.

In order to say *He is singing*, the Hebrew participle needs a self-standing subject pronoun. "I am going to him" is a case in point, but in *he will not come back*, the verb has the subject *he* built into it, but the pronoun *he* has been added. Thus a deliberate contrast between *I* and *he* is intended here, a contrast we have attempted to reproduce by translating the clause as "it is I that am going to him." Moreover, this was not said by David in the manner of a Christian saying to someone about to breathe his or her last: "I am coming to you soon." One is rather reminded of the description of Abraham's death: "Abraham breathed his last and died in good old age .. and was gathered to his people (i.e. his already deceased forefathers)" (Gn 25.8). We do not think that David believed in a life after death. When Jesus comforted Martha over the death of her brother Lazarus, saying "he will rise again," she said: "I do know that, at the time of resurrection on the last day, he will rise again" (Joh 11.24). She appears to be a step or two ahead of David.

8) Finale: Part II, "Like father, like son"[9] (2Sm 13.1-39)

"This is a sequel to the preceding story. Absalom, a son of David's, had a beautiful sister, Tamar by name, and Amnon, a son of David's, fell in love with her." (vs. 1)

The Greek translation reads: "a very good-looking sister," with two extra words, what probably stood in the Qumran Hebrew fragment as well. Exactly as in the case of their step-mother, uncommon beauty is going to play a vital role in the story about to unfold itself, not the woman's personality or character.

---

[9] Cf. "Like mother, like daughter" (Ezk 16.44).

Later we are going to take a close look at the notion of love in the Bible (pp. 89ff.). The verb translated above with "fell in love" is also sometimes rendered with "loved." Vs. 15 tells us that, after Amnon had raped Tamar, his hatred for her was stronger than the love he earlier felt for her, which suggests what kind of love is being talked about here. This Hebrew word was not used in the preceding two chapters. Amnon's father lusted after Bathsheba.

"Amnon found himself in a tight corner, so much so that he pretended to be ill. Since she was a virgin, it appeared to Amnon that there was not a thing he could do." (vs. 2)

From "it appeared to Amnon" one can conclude that here is presented his own view, not the author's. The reason for his dilemma was Tamar's virginity. We see that it had not occurred to him that, even if she was a half-sister, incest was a dreadful sin. Even so, it is a redeeming factor that, at this stage, he still retained some sense of moral propriety.

The Hebrew verb for 'to pretend to be ill' recurs in vs. 5 and 6. In vs. 5 Jonadab advises Amnon to do so, which he does (vs. 6). At vs. 2, however, many translate it as "he became ill," "he fell sick," etc. Though the form of the verb as used here, in theory, could mean 'to become ill, fall sick'[10], its use in a significantly different sense with the same actor in this proximity sounds a little unlikely. If Amnon had been genuinely ill on his friend's daily visits, he would not have advised Amnon to feign to be ill. He had become love-sick. He looked sick, as Qimhi, a mediaeval Jewish commentator, justly notes; he looked in low spirits, depressed. Our author then is already having the whole progression of the story in purview, a discourse technique which we noticed earlier with reference to Gn 22.1 (p. 25). Right at the start of the story the heinous nature of Amnon's deed is underlined and the ultimate responsibility is squarely laid at his door, and not that of his friend.

"³Amnon had a friend, Jonadab by name, a son of Shima, a brother of David's. Jonadab was very clever. ⁴Jonadab said to him: 'Why, o

---

[10] On my enquiry, Mr Richard Medina, an acquaintance of mine in Jerusalem, has told me that the first instance of such a usage occurs in a Hebrew document composed sometime between the 7th and 8th century. It is then more likely an innovation than a sudden emergence of a usage that lay hidden more than a millennium.

Prince, are you so sombre morning after morning? Wouldn't you tell me?' Amnon said to him: 'I'm in love with Tamar, a sister of Absalom's, my brother.'" (vs. 3-4)

The Hebrew adjective translated here as "clever" is a most common word, also meaning 'wise.' However, one doubts that his advice is illustrative of wisdom God would approve of. Our author is unlikely suggesting that Jonadab was generally wise, but this time went a bit astray.

"⁵Jonadab said to him: 'Lie in your bed and pretend to be ill. Then your father will he coming to see you, and then say to him: "Please let Tamar my sister come to me, cook a meal for me, and dress the food in my sight so that I can watch and eat it from her hand." ' ⁶Amnon lay (in his bed), pretending to be ill. The king came to see him, and Amnon said to the king: 'Please let Tamar my sister come and make two cakes in my sight for me to eat (them) from her hand'. ⁷David sent a message to Tamar at home: 'Go, please, to the house of Amnon your brother and cook some food for him.'" (vs. 5-7)

Earlier we discussed the root of the verb rendered here with 'to lie (in bed)' (pp. 37f.). The translator responsible for the Old Greek appears to be commendably sensitive to the choice of Greek verbs. The one chosen here simply means 'to lie in bed to sleep at night or for an afternoon nap,' different from the one chosen in the preceding two chapters, where it refers to what a male and a female do in bed. Our translator knew of course what use Amnon was going to put the bed to, but he probably thought that its use here was premature. He would select it when he comes to vs. 11.

"And she took the plate, poured (sauce) in his presence, but he refused to eat. Amnon said: 'Everyone out off me!,' and everyone went out off him." (vs. 9)

The Old Greek says: 'he kept refusing.' Tamar kept urging him to eat what she had cooked.

The word translated here as "out" is an imperative verb in the plural, "Get out!". Tamar was probably being helped by two or more servants. The same imperative form had been used by Joseph hundreds of years before, because he feared that he might not be able to control his emotions when he was going to disclose his identity to his brothers (Gn 45.1), and he did not want that to be witnessed by strangers. This time, however, Amnon's motive was elsewhere.

"And Amnon said to Tamar: 'Bring the food to the room. I like to eat it from your hand. And Tamar took the cakes which she had cooked and brought them to Amnon her brother to the room." (vs. 10).

The Hebrew word for "room" here has the definite article. The kitchen was probably adjoining his room, the door of which was ajar so that he could watch as she cooked, and she knew which room he was referring to.

"And she took it to him for him to eat, but he grabbed her, saying to her: 'Come in, lie with me, sister!'" (vs. 11).

The verb translated above as "come in" can also mean just 'come.' But she was already standing at his bedside with his meal, so that he is most likely urging her to get into his bed.

   "Lie with me!" was also said by the wife of Potiphar, a high-ranking officer in the Pharaonic court (Gn 39.7). Her request was turned down. That was the first case of a rape attempted by a female in the history of mankind.

   The Old Greek lacks 'sister.' The translator may not have wanted her to be so addressed in this context.

"And she said to him: 'No, brother. Don't humiliate me. For no such thing is to be done in Israel. Don't commit this villainy." (vs. 12)

The verb translated above "humiliate" is often used with reference to rape, e.g. Dt 22.24, Jdg 19.24. The first instance is Gn 34.2, where Dinah, whom Leah bore to Jacob, was deflowered by Schechem, a Hivite; Hivites were already settled in Canaan when Abraham arrived there.

   The root of this Hebrew verb often carries the sense of 'low': in social status or 'poor' in financial terms, and also 'humble' in moral character. Having fasted forty days and forty nights in the wilderness of Judaea and having been challenged by the devil, 'if you are the son of God, turn these stones into bread,' Jesus quoted 'Man shall not live by bread alone, but by every word of God that issues forth from His mouth' (Dt 8.3). He knew of course that this quote is immediately preceded by 'and He humbled you, made you feel hungry, fed you with manna .. in order to let you know that not on bread alone man shall live ...'.

The verb translated as "humbled" is the same as that used by Tamar. We are dependent on God not only for our spiritual survival, but also for physical, bodily; see above at p. 45. It is interesting that a noun from the same root, / ta'anít/, is used in the sense of 'fasting' at Ezr 9.5.[11]

Raped women often find themselves at the bottom rang of their society, are looked down as rubbish, wooed by nobody. Of victims who had survived the war as sexual slaves of the Japanese Army there were many who thought that they couldn't possibly go home, and took their own lives. Even some who braved and returned home would remain silent, taking their memories with them on their death. That is why so few are officially recognised as former "comfort women" in many Asian countries. The Septuagint uses a verb which, when translated literally, means 'to lower,' which is precisely what sexual abuse and rape mean. For it is not only physical violence, but also denigration of human dignity. Recently, when a South Korean diplomat referred to Korean "comfort women" as sex slaves, the Japanese Government protested against this as going against the agreement reached in 2015 between the two governments. What do current officials of the Japanese Government think of those wartime Korean women who were, against their will, forced to satisfy sexual desires of Japanese soldiers? Such Japanese public servants are not much different from Japanese right-wingers who unashamedly assert that those victims were just prostitutes after money.

The Hebrew word, /nvalá/, translated above as "villainy," denotes an act of open disregard of moral and religious codes of behaviour, and often is applied to cases of sexual abuse, though not consistently.[12] In Jdg 19 we read a horrid story of a man who went to Bethlehem to bring back a runaway concubine of his. On their way home, when they reached Gibeah, the night fell and they were getting ready to sleep rough on a street. Then a local old man offered them accommodation for the night. Whilst they were enjoying an evening meal, a group of local rogues arrived and demanded for the guest to be brought out so that they could have fun with him. Horrified, the host offered his daughter and the guest's concubine, but asked the guys not to commit such a wanton deed against his guest. The Hebrew word used here and that describing what the men did to the two females are the same as those used by Tamar. One wonders whether in this part of Israel raping was tolerable at the time, but not sodomy.

---

[11] At Ps 35.13 and Is 58.3, 5, for instance, this verb occurs alongside a word explicitly denoting fast.

[12] At 1Sm 25.25 Abigail pleads with David to pay no regard to her husband, who she says is true to his name, /navál/. The same word is also used to indicate what some soldiers under the command of Joshua did; in breach of God's command they could not resist the attraction of the spoils of enemies (Josh 7.15).

"Where can I take this disgrace to? You will become one of the villains in Israel. Now, please speak to the king, for he wouldn't withhold me from you'." (vs. 13)

Here again the self-standing personal pronouns for *I* and *you* are deliberately added, and both up front. The one emphasises Tamar's despair, and the other her desperate attempt to dissuade her brother.

The question put by Tamar is worded in a most painful, heart-breaking manner in the Old Greek: "Is there any place where my disgrace would not reach?" She being a princess, this horrid story would follow her wherever she might turn. Wherever she settles, she would have to live away from inquisitive eyes of curiosity.

The suggestion made by Tamar presents a difficult problem for Old Testament scholars. Even with a half-brother or a half-sister, sexual intercourse is forbidden. See Lv 18.9, for instance. However, Abraham admitted openly that Sarah was a half-sister (Gn 20.12). Laws and regulations in Ancient Israel may have changed with the passage of time. Even so, what Amnon was about to do before marriage was unlawful, a case of rape and sexual abuse.

"But he wouldn't listen to her. He overpowered her, humiliated her, and forced an intercourse on her." (vs. 14)

The verb translated here as "overpowered" shares the same root as that for "grabbed" (vs. 11). Tamar protested not only verbally,[13] but perhaps also physically struggled with him, slapping him on the face, kicking at his legs, and so on. Alas she was no match for him.

The last verb of the verse is a keyword in this whole saga, and we have translated it with 'to lie with' at 2Sm 11.4. There it may not have been a case of rape (see above at pp. 39f.), but here it certainly is. "Lay with her" might sound a bit too neutral.

"[15]Amnon felt great hatred for her. The hatred he felt for her was more intense than the love he (initially) had for her, and he said to her, 'Up, get lost!' [16]Tamar said to him. 'No way, brother. This second evil of

---

[13] A former colleague of mine at Leiden University, Dr Fokkelman, justly notes: "like his father," who ignored an alarm-bell ringing loud and clear, when informed by his servants that the beautiful woman he had spied from the roof of his royal suite was a married woman.

sending me away is graver than the first you have done to me.' But he refused to listen to her." (vs. 15-16)

The first half of vs. 16 in the traditional Hebrew text appears to be considerably amiss. The above-given translation is based on the Qumran fragment, with which the Septuagint largely agrees.

At this stage Tamar may not have been betrothed to anyone. Nor do we know whether she was aware of an old regulation that prescribes that a male who has raped such a woman is obliged to pay her father a fair sum, marry her and shall not be allowed to divorce her all his life (Ex 22.15, Dt 22.28-29), but her remark is absolutely right. In any case that was the minimum of compensation the perpetrator should make. Otherwise the victim will be treated as unqualified for marriage, will not enjoy the pleasure of motherhood, and will have no choice but to make a living all on herself for her whole life.

"And he called a young servant of his and said: 'Get this out off me, and lock the door behind her!'" (vs. 17)

The Hebrew word for "servant" here is in the singular, though the imperative "Get out" is in the plural. Did Amnon fear that she might put up too violent a struggle for one servant to handle? But in vs. 18 only one servant managed to do it. The plural imperative is longer than the singular by one letter only, so that a scribal error is more likely.

The Hebrew demonstrative pronoun for "this" is sometimes used with a nuance of disgust and contempt: "this bitch"?

The Hebrew for "off me" here is, literally translated, 'from on me.' Tamar was felt to be a burden stuck on him.

In "Get me off" a verb is used of the same root as in "send me away" said by Tamar. For Amnon the operation may have been nothing but physically moving her out, but the form she used is the same as in "to divorce" mentioned above (Dt 22.28-29).

"She was wearing a garment reaching down to her ankles. Virgin princesses would wear such coats. His servant took her out, locking the door behind her." (vs. 18)

The Hebrew phrase rendered as "a garment reaching down to ankles" is also used of what Jacob had made for Joseph, his favourite son (Gn 37.3). Here it is symbolic of a high rank, whereas Joseph showed it off and aroused his brothers' intense jealousy and hatred. Precisely what the Hebrew phrase means is still debated. Ancient Greek translators must have known its Septuagint translation at Gn 37.3 in the sense of 'multi-coloured coat,' but their successors decided not to adopt it. The Hebrew phrase occurs only twice in the Bible. The Old Greek has 'a garment reaching down to ankles,'[14] whereas the newer version has 'a garment reaching down to wrists.' Ladies' fashions may have changed with the passage of time just as today. Once a mini was alright for a princess, but later she was allowed to have her legs exposed, but not her arms.

"And Tamar grabbed some ashes, spreading them on her head, the garment reaching down to her ankles she was wearing she tore, she put her hands on her head and walked on and on, as she cried aloud." (vs. 19)

Tearing of one's garment is a symbolic expression of grief. So does David on hearing that all his princes had been murdered at Absalom's hands (vs. 31). What Tamar tore was not only a gorgeous garment of a princess, but also a symbol of a virgin.

Reading on till the end of Chapter 19 one gets the impression that here is a piece of Greek tragedy being played out before us, a baneful /móira/ 'fate' being passed down from one generation to another, striking down one sibling after another. What David did with Bathsheba was its ultimate, root cause. The first victim was a prince to die too young even to be given a name. David wept, as he stood beside the baby whose chance of survival receded minute after minute. The second victim ravaged by a horrid rape wailed aloud within hearing of many people around. Then follows the death of another prince, which David, if only he had so willed, could have averted. At his death, all that the father was capable of was to tear his own clothes out of grief and lie on the ground (vs. 31). This tragic sequence of deaths climaxed with that of Absalom, the king's beloved son. On hearing the glad tidings of the defeat of the coup d'état headed by Absalom, the king nervously asked, "Is Absalom the lad OK?" The herald, not daring to give a straight answer, could only reply evasively: "May your enemies, sir, become like that lad, and all who have rebelled against you be doomed!" Understanding the message, "the king was deeply shaken, went up to the attic above the gate and wept. This is what he said, as he walked: 'My son, Absalom, my son, my son, Absalom, How much better would it have been

---

[14] This appears to have been acceptable to Josephus, a Jewish historian of the early Christian era, who was conversant with Hebrew, Aramaic, and Greek.

for me to die in your stead, Absalom, my son, my son!'" (2Sm 18.32-19.1). He repeated 'Absalom' three times, and 'my son' five times. This heart-wrenching cry must have echoed throughout the city. The herald reported to Joab that the king was crying, mourning over Absalom.

The Bible keeps quiet as to whether or not Tamar became pregnant. Even if she did, she wouldn't have raised a *cri de joie*. One who caught the dying Ishmael's inaudible cry couldn't have failed to hear the grievous cry of Tamar ringing all round, and may have seen to it that she wouldn't have to cry over a prince doomed to die anonymous.

On the coffin of Achiram, the king of Phoenicia, there are painted women lamenting his death with their hands laid not on their chests, but on their heads.

"And Absalom her brother said to her: 'Aminon your brother was with you? Now, sister, keep quiet. He's your brother. Don't pay attention to this matter. And Tamar stayed at Absalom, her brother's home, dazed." (vs. 20)

In the Hebrew original, the question put by Absalom sounds innocent, but it is most unlikely that he didn't know what had happened. The Greek translator apparently sensed it, as shown by the question worded as a rhetorical one: "Amnon, your brother, wasn't with you, was he?" Absalom was probably doing his best to empathise with her, but in vain. His true perspective is betrayed in his contemptuous 'Aminon,' i.e. 'that infantile Amnon.'[15] The situation is a grave one, since he speaks of 'your brother,' when he should have said 'my brother.'

'For a man to be with a woman' or the other way round is a euphemism for sexual intercourse, as it is said that, when Potiphar's wife tried to seduce Joseph, he refused 'to be with her' (Gn 39.10), whereas in lying to her folks, she was straightforward, saying "he invaded my room to have sex with me" (vs. 14).

The word translated above with "dazed" means 'abandoned, receiving no care and attention.' The Old Greek says: "living as a widow and dejected." The translator may have thought that just one word could hardly do justice to the bottomless depression to which she had been abandoned by Amnon. When this Greek version came into being, the project of translating the book of Isaiah may not have got off the ground yet. The Hebrew word we find here is used in "a woman abandoned by her husband has more kids than a woman still with a husband" (Is 54.1).

---

[15] /aminón/ is intended to marginalise /amnón/.

"And David the king heard all this story and became very angry."
(vs. 21)

The word order of the first clause is analogous to that we noted at Gn 22.1, i.e.
<subject – verb – object> (p. 25). It is not just recording in chronological sequence
what happened after what is related in the preceding verse. It forms a bridge
between the preceding story and the new tragedy about to be recounted; it introduces the background of the new story. Our author may be wanting to say that the
root cause of the tragedy about to unfold itself lies in the fact that David's reaction
at the knowledge of this domestic wickedness stopped at anger. Shouldn't he have
summoned Amnon, remonstrated with him, and demanded that he take Tamar for
a wife? The Hebrew for "became angry" is very similar to that used in describing
David's initial reaction on hearing Nathan's parable (2Sm 12.5). The context is
so similar between the two, but David's reactions are vastly different. The Old
Greek offers a rather unusual rendition: "he became depressed, despondent." This
is all the more striking, since at 2Sm 12.5 he chose a standard translation, "he
became angry." Noting that the king's anger did not lead to any further action, he
may deliberately have chosen this extraordinary translation.

It is a lull before a storm. On the surface the palace was all quiet. The father
remained reticent, the whereabouts of the perpetrator were unknown, the victim's brother advised her to keep quiet and not make a fuss about the matter,
and she, grateful for her brother's concern, followed his advice. In the remainder
of the verse both Greek versions provide an excuse for the king's inaction: "but
he did not cause pain to the heart of Amnon, his son, because he loved him; he
was his eldest son." Since the Qumran fragment also preserves this addition
more or less, it must have dropped out for some reason or other. If it had been
a genuine love, the father should have seen to it that his son felt pain in his heart.

Our Greek translators most likely knew that the Hebrew verb used here for
love has a rather broad range. At the start of this chapter it is used to indicate
Amnon's momentary lust. They probably knew also that in Gn 37 this verb
indicates Jacob's favouritism, that the Septuagint uses the same verb as that
being used here (see pp. 91f. below), and also that favouritism and partiality
brought about a series of tragedies one after another.

"Absalom did not speak to Amnon at all; Absalom hated Amnon on
account of the fact that he had humiliated Tamar his sister." (vs. 22)

The Hebrew for "at all" here is "(starting) from good and (finishing at) bad."
When the brothers ran into each other on the palace grounds, they may have

said "Hello," but would not touch on anything that has to do with ethics or morality. Such an analysis is not impossible, but the idiom is used as an expression of total, absolute negation with no moral, ethical nuances, e.g. "Take heed that you do not argue with Jacob at all" (Gn 31.24).

"²³Now it was two years after that they were shearing sheep for Absalom in Baalhazor near Ephraim, and Absalom invited all the princes. ²⁴And Absalom came to the king and said: 'Behold, they are shearing my sheep now. May Your Majesty and His servants come with your servant!'" (vs. 23-24)

The end of this important event in the agricultural calendar was about to be celebrated in a grand style.

The Septuagint has "after as many as two years," emphasising the length of time that had elapsed since the tragedy and how long Absalom had agonised before deciding to act. In the meantime the matter must have come up between him and his sister many a time. A few years later he would get a daughter, also beautiful, whom he would name Tamar (2Sm 14.27), showing how deeply he was attached to his sister.

For *my* and *me* in Absalom's invitation Hebrew has 'your servant,' and for *your* it has 'his.' This is typical of the etiquette of courteous discourse observed in Biblical Hebrew. In Japanese a student says to his teacher: "Is the teacher coming?" instead of "Are you coming?". Even a prince is seen as keeping a respectful distance towards his father.[16]

"²⁵The king said to Absalom: 'No, son. We would not go all of us together and be a burden on you.' He [= Absalom] pressed him, but he refused to go, saying "Have a good day!" ²⁶Absalom said: 'If so, then let Amnon my brother go with us!' Then the king said to him:

[16] In the seventies of the last century I watched a then popular American film, *Love story*. It was about a Harvard student who fell in love with a girl student at a neighbouring college. They decide to marry, and visit his father at home. In speaking to his father the student addresses him with *Sir*, not *Dad* or *Daddy*, which was an eye-opener for me, for my image of America was a country where, after an initial introduction, you begin to address your new acquaintance with his or her first name. See "Yes, sir," a son replying to his father (Mt 21.30). Literally translated the word means 'Lord.' In Japanese even a senior person keeps a distance: "Do you understand what the teacher [= *I*] is saying to you?" A biblical example is "Share your master's [= *my*] joy!" (Mt 25.21).

'Why should he go with you?'. [27]Absalom pressed him and he [= the king] let Amnon and all the princes go with him." (vs. 25-27)

A literal rendition of the end of vs. 25 is "and he blessed him."

According to vs. 23 Absalom had sent an invitation to all the princes, among whom Amnon would be included. The king may have been aware that Amnon had declined to go. In vs. 26 Absalom uses the plural form, 'with us,' but the king's 'with you' is in the singular. He may have guessed what Absalom was up to.

In both of the Greek versions vs. 27 ends with "and Absalom threw a party in the style of a royal party." It is well known that, when two adjoining clauses begin or end with an identical word or phrase, the eyes of a scribe may skip and inadvertently let the immediately following or preceding words drop. Here, too, the traditional text ends with "the king" and in the Hebrew text used by the Greek translators the following clause is likely to have ended with "the king."[17] David may have felt uneasy with him only being absent, and encouraged Absalom to throw a respectable gala at his [= David's] expenses.

"Absalom commanded his subordinates: 'Do look! When Amnon begins to feel good with wine, I shall say to you: "Attack Amnon and kill him!" Don't be scared. It's me that am giving this order. Be courageous, and be warriors!'" (vs. 28)

"It's me" is an attempt to reproduce the emphatic force of the seemingly redundant Hebrew pronoun for *I* here. Absalom is emphasising that he will take all the responsibility for the intended outcome. His attitude is slightly different from that displayed by his father. But why wouldn't Absalom do it himself? Had David told him what he had heard through Nathan? "Why have you struck Uriah the Hittite …? Why have you taken his wife for a wife of your own? Why did you kill him with the sword of Ammonites?" (2Sm 12.9) If Absalom had intended to attack other princes as well, he might have needed to be helped by his subordinates. Is he not, precisely like his father, trying to achieve his end through accomplices? Isn't he being as despicable as his father? His father had his loyal soldier, who was battling, risking his life, killed by enemies Uriah was fighting against.

In "Attack Amnon and kill him!" only the first Hebrew verb is imperative, and the second indicates a subsequent action distinct from the first. If Amnon, having been attacked with a sword or a spear, is still breathing, they are to finish

---

[17] One of the Qumran fragments, 4QSam[a], has preserved some traces of this missing clause.

him off. In a description of a context similar to the one here we observe an analogous Hebrew structure. When David decided to have Uriah disposed of, he instructed Joab to see to it that his soldiers take Uriah to a perilous spot in the battlefield, abandon him there, and withdraw so that he would be struck and die (2Sm 11.15), where only the first verb is imperative.[18]

"29Absalom's subordinates did to Amnon as Absalom had ordered. Then all the princes got up and each mounted his mule and fled. 30Whilst they were still on the way, a report reached David: 'Absalom has attacked all the princes and none of them has survived.'" (vs. 29-30)

The grammatical form of the verb rendered here "reached" indicates that the princes running for their lives had been preceded by a herald carrying a wrong message. David, who had posted security staff at various places to watch Uriah's every single movement in Jerusalem, may have become suspicious of this feast and have had a secret agent at the gala party. When the attack on Amnon began, the agent got frightened and, without ascertaining the situation accurately and thinking that the other princes were also in danger, dashed out instantly. He may have had a means of transport faster than a mule.

"David got up, tore his garments, and lay on the ground. All his servants were standing by with their garments torn." (vs. 31)

The key verb of this whole saga (2Sm 11-13), /shakháv/, used to describe what David did night after night beside the critically ill baby born from Bathsheba (2Sm 12.16), is used here as well in "lay on the ground." This came over him, because Amnon, his son, lay (/shakháv/) with Tamar.

David performs three actions in quick succession: "got up, tore, lay." On the herald's arrival he may have been seated on the throne and it may have been easier to tear the garments, standing. However, the Hebrew verb for 'get up' does not necessarily imply that someone was seated until then, but can be used with a nuance of decisive or non-hesitant action. Followed by an imperative,

---

[18] An alternative grammatical analysis would take the verb for "kill him" as continuing that for "I shall say": if the soldiers had executed as commanded, Amnon's death would have already become a reality. The verb translated here as 'attack' often means 'to deal a fatal blow.' But in 2Sm 11.15 the verb has the victim as its grammatical subject, whereas here the subject is plural, attackers. Then the first analysis might deserve preference.

"Go!," the person may already have been standing. When Jacob, carrying a cooked meal, came into Isaac's tent, and said, "Please get up, sit, and eat," his father was not necessarily in need of physical exercise. In "Up, get lost!" (vs. 15) the two imperatives follow each other: literally rendered, 'Get up, go!'. Tamar may have been overpowered by Amnon and still lying in bed.

"Jonadab, a son of Shima, a brother of David's, having understood the situation, said: 'You should not think that they have slaughtered all the young princes, but only Amnon is dead. Since the day when Amnon humiliated Tamar his sister, Absalom kept mentioning the matter." (vs. 32)

The Hebrew verb rendered as "having understood" means literally 'he answered,' but Jonadab had not been asked a question. The word sometimes means 'to observe a situation and orally react.'

The Hebrew text translated above as "Absalom kept mentioning the matter" still remains the bane of biblical scholars. Every time Absalom met his dear friend, the matter was likely on his lips. But two years long! That is a very long time indeed. Before suggesting that he should have left that painful past behind and moved forward, we should do our best to appreciate his unfathomable pain and agony he was not able to face and handle that long.

"Therefore, do not think at all, sir, that all the princes have died, for Amnon alone has died!" (vs. 33)

The rendition "at all" reproduces a Hebrew word meaning 'word' or 'matter.' When it is used, as here, without the definite article and with a negative particle, it stresses the notion of negation: 'nothing, nothing whatsoever, not a word, not at all.' It cannot thus mean 'the matter, the report' as found in some translations.

"Absalom fled. A young guard raised his eyes and saw, and there was a large crowd walking along the path of Horonayim on the descent. The guard came and told the king: 'I saw people from the path of Horonayim, from the mountain.'" (vs. 34)

That the traditional text is in a chaotic state is generally recognised. The translation offered above is based on what was reconstructed, by taking the later Septuagint into account, by J. Wellhausen, an outstanding German biblical scholar (1844-1918). The people spotted by the guard were walking, hence not the princes fleeing on the mules' backs. At a grand festive occasion there must have been quite a few people, such as waiters and waitresses, in addition to Absalom's subordinates who attacked Amnon.

When the guard reported to the king about his sighting people, the Old Greek uses a construction meaning "I did see indeed," implying that the report was an eye-witness account, not a rumour.

"³⁵*Jonadab said to the king: 'Here are the princes just arrived. It has happened just as I have said (to you, sir).' ³⁶When he finished speaking, behold the princes arrived and they lifted their voice and wept. Also the king and all his servants wept their hearts out very bitterly."* (vs. 35-36)

The end of vs. 35 is an idiomatic rendition for "as said by your servant."

The extraordinary intensity of their emotions is indicated in three manners in the Hebrew text of the end of vs. 36.

"³⁷*In the meantime Absalom had fled and gone to Talmai, a son of Amihud, the king of Geshur and he [= David] mourned over his son the whole of this period. ³⁸In the meantime Absalom had fled and gone to Geshur, and he was there three years. David the king lost the will power for going at Absalom, for he had come to terms with Amnon's death."* (vs. 37-39)

To mention the flight of Absalom three times (vs. 34, 37, 38) might strike us as odd. However, in the last two cases the word order is changed, a sequence that provides the background for what is about to be told. Hence our insertion of 'in the meantime.'

The problematic nature of vs. 39 in the traditional Hebrew text has been generally known. The first verb is a feminine form in spite of the fact that David is its subject. This enigma has been happily resolved through a Qumran fragment (4QSamᵃ) which has preserved traces of a noun of feminine gender, a noun meaning 'spirit.' Since both of the Greek versions use here a noun which is a common translation of the Hebrew word in question, this must be a scribal error due to the scribe responsible for the traditional Hebrew text. Scribes of the Bible were all properly trained and experienced, but they are also human after all and rare slips are understandable.[19]

---

[19] As an example of those scribes' professional dedication we may mention that, at the end of the book of Deuteronomy, we read a scribal note saying "the total number of verses of this book

We would like to conclude this extended study of 2Sm 11-13 by quoting what Bar Efrat, an Israeli scholar, has said: "The murder is a punishment for Amnon … and likewise a punishment for David for his murder of Uriah .., just as the rape of Tamar was a punishment for David for his deed against Bath-sheba."

is 955, that of the Torah, i.e. the entire Pentateuch, 5,849, the total number of words in the Torah 79,856, the total number of letters in the Torah 400,945." We are provided with comparable data on the rest of the Old Testament, showing that these scribes, on completing copying one book, went back to its Chapter 1, Verse 1, and manually counted everything to ensure that not a verse, not a word, not a letter has fallen out. These are kinds of statistics which you can obtain these days in a second or two by pressing a few keys on your computer.

CHAPTER II

GREEK

A) Personal pronouns

The verb in all the three biblical languages has an element built into its form and shows whether the person or thing that does, did, or will do something is *I*, *we* (first person), *you* (second person), or *he*, *she*, *it*, *they* (third person). In many languages, however, these pronouns are self-standing words separate from their verbs. Hence, *I went*, *you went*, *she went* and so on. In Greek, for instance, *I baptise* is /baptízo:/, *we baptise* is /baptízomen/; the two forms share /baptíz-/. The addition of such a separate pronoun indicates focus on the person indicated with it. When John the Baptist introduced himself with "*I* baptise you with water for repentance. He who comes after me is mightier than I" (Mt 3.11), the special pronoun indicates that John was conscious of his subordinate status and mission. In his sermon on the mount Jesus said to His audience: "*You* are the salt of the earth .. *you* are the light of the world" (Mt 5.13-14). He was highlighting the unique mission of the audience, nobody else can or must carry out such a mission. When Jesus said before His ascension "*I* am with you all the time till the end of this world" (Mt 28.20), it must have sounded truly reassuring to His disciples, who had barely recovered from their shock over the recent crucifixion of their master, but none other than He who had risen from the dead pledged to go along with them all the way. This is different from "Where two or three are gathered in My name, there I am in their midst" (Mt 18.20), where no separate pronoun for *I* is used. Nor do we find a personal pronoun used in "He has trusted God. Let Him rescue now, if He still accepts him, for He said 'I am a son of God'" (Mt 27.43), where the Jewish leaders are mocking Jesus. Whereas the orthodox Christian doctrine says that Jesus alone can make a claim to divinity, that is not a position the mockers are attributing to Jesus hanging on the cross, but they were of the opinion that Jesus claimed to be semi-divine. The definite article is significantly absent in the Greek text from the noun translated here 'son.' Hebrew and Aramaic are slightly different from Greek in this respect. When Jacob was asked by Isaac his father "Who are you, my son?" (Gn 27.18), where Isaac is trying to establish which of his twin sons is there, there is no verb in Jacob's answer "I am Esau your eldest son." Hebrew, however, can vary the relative sequence of the two core words: either *I* first, /ano<u>kh</u>í ya'aqóv/ or *I* second, /ya'aqóv ano<u>kh</u>í/. By selecting the first, Jacob unwittingly betrayed his dark design, for the first sequence lays emphasis on the pronoun. I am sceptical that Jesus conversed and taught in Greek. In some of the examples cited above Jesus may have used this sequence. In a language such as English one could italicise the pronoun, e.g. '*You* are the salt of the earth' or pronounce it with a raised pitch.[1] Jesus declared aspects of His unique mission by the formula *I am so and so*. This is particularly prominent in the fourth Gospel, occurring as many as fourteen times. E.g. "I am the bread of life" (6.48), "I am the good shepherd" (10.11), "I am the way, the truth, and the life. Unless via me nobody can come to the Father" (14.6).

B) The definite article

Some languages in the world lack the definite article, *the* in English.

Some years ago I taught an intensive five-week beginners' course in New Testament Greek at a theological seminary in Kota Kinabalu in Borneo. The subject was obligatory, and some students were finding it rather demanding. When we were on to the definite article, I said: "Half of you are Chinese-speaking and the other half are Malay-speaking. Neither language has the definite article. Right? When you were taught English at high-school, you must have struggled hard, trying to know when to say *the book, the books*, or just *a book, books*. The Greek definite article has as many as twenty-four forms, all of which can be translated as *the*. I do appreciate your frustration."[2] Among the select passages we read in Greek, there was the parable of the prodigal son (Lk 15.11-32). When we came to a description of the father spotting one day his son still at a distance, taking pity on him, dashing outdoors, hugging and kissing him (verse 20), I pointed out that the Greek verb often translated "took pity" can best be translated with a Classical Chinese expression consisting of four Chinese characters. This idiomatic expression is based on an ancient story in the Chinese classics about a famous

---

[1] When it is concerned with a verb other than one that indicates existence or equation, Hebrew and Aramaic do not differ from Greek, which applies also when the Hebrew or Aramaic verb *be* is in the past or future tense.

[2] I could appreciate their position as a native speaker of Japanese, which lacks the definite article as well.

warrior-statesman Kangwong of Jin (312-73). He went on a long journey. A servant of his spotted a baby monkey on the way and caught it just for fun for the long
journey. The mother monkey kept following them about 400 km along the coast
and eventually managed to get on their boat, but she was exhausted and dropped
dead. When the servant cut her up, he saw all her intestines shredded into tiny
pieces, all out of her profound love and affection for her baby. My students were
delighted. The Chinese speakers among them exclaimed: "Professor, if by reading
this story in Greek we can appreciate it in such depth, we are going to study this
evening all the 24 forms of the definite article!"

Incidentally, the Greek verb /splangkhnízomai/ in question in the parable of the
prodigal son occurs a total of 12 times in the New Testament, and that in the
synoptic Gospels. Except this case and another in the parable of a good Samaritan
also told by Jesus (Lk 10.33) it is always used to refer to emotions that arose in
the heart of Jesus confronted by some painful sight and as perceived by the three
Gospel writers with one exception in Mk 8.2 and its parallel in Mt 15.32, where
Jesus Himself uses the verb, facing a crowd who had been listening to His teaching with profound interest for three days, giving a miss to their meals. As He told
the parable of the prodigal son and that of a good Samaritan, He may have been
feeling strong empathy towards the father and the Samaritan respectively.

Some time ago I was asked by a Japanese high-school student about "The truth
will set you free" (Joh 8.32). She wondered what truth has got to do with freedom.
I replied: "You are reading the Bible in Japanese, which has no definite article.
But the Greek word for 'truth' here does have it, and Jesus was talking about a
specific kind of truth; He would later say 'I am the way, the truth, and the life'
(Joh 14.6)." After having mailed to her, I remembered the famous question put
by Pontius Pilate: "What is truth?" (Joh 18.38). I discovered for the first time
that the Greek word for 'truth' there has no definite article, although Pilate's
question was evoked by what Jesus had said: "I have come to the world in order
to testify to the truth, and whoever is of the truth will listen to what I say"
(verse37). I suppose that Pilate knew no Hebrew or Aramaic and had an interpreter seated next to him, and the interpreter mechanically translated into Latin,
which has no definite article, so that Pilate ended up asking an abstract, philosoph-
ical question. Having heard the question translated back into Hebrew or Aramaic
without the article, Jesus may have concluded: "This fellow has no ear for what
I could say to him further."[3] I for one would not castigate Him for throwing to
the wind the golden chance of making the first Roman Christian.

---

[3] A brief study of mine arising from this experience has been published in *Biblica* 99 (2018)
117-18: "Truth or the truth?".

C) Past, Present, Future

The logical categories of past, present, and future may be universal and known to any culture. However, their linguistic expression is not uniform and differs from language to language. Japanese, for instance, manages basically with two forms: past and non-past. Chinese is extreme in this regard. Its verbs mark no time distinction at all, for such a differentiation is left to the general context or to specific words or phrases such as *yesterday, at this moment, tomorrow.*

In addition to this tense opposition, Greek, like some other languages, knows a category called aspect. It comes in three varieties: Present, Perfect, and Aorist [= 'indeterminate']. The Present aspect views an action in its progression; features such as repetitive, ongoing, habitual are marked with this aspect. A verb in the Perfect aspect indicates that an action that took place prior to the moment of speech or writing is currently complete and finished. The Aorist aspect is used in order to indicate an action in itself with no reference to its progression or completion. As such it can indicate not only an action that took place in the past, but also an action currently going on.

As if this were not enough, Greek, like some other languages, marks the feature of voice such as active and passive, and mood such as indicative, subjunctive, and optative. The feature of aspect applies also to the infinitive, participle, and imperative. If you add all this to the features of number (singular and plural) and person (*I, you, he* etc.), one Greek verb can have up to 680 different variants. It's maddening! This, however, does not make Greeks a nation of geniuses. If you start learning Greek as a baby from your mother, you will eventually master it, even before you go to a kindergarten. Such a kid will not have heard of tense, aspect etc. Yet it will know when to use an Aorist form, not a Perfect form. Very few students at Greek universities would be able to answer a foreigner why an Aorist form, not a Present form, is used in any specific case.

Given the fundamental importance of these categories of the Greek verb system, we shall study them with reference to some concrete examples, and not in terms of abstract, theoretical categories.

C 1) A sinful woman (Lk 7.36-50)

Jesus was invited by a certain Pharisee for a dinner. The aspect of the verb used here is Present. The Pharisee sent the invitation more than once. Jesus was too busy or initially did not feel like it.

An anonymous woman who was contemptuously known to the townsfolk as 'sinner' got the wind of Jesus being at the Pharisee's, hurried to his house, and sneaked in. Then what does she do?

"Having taken her position behind Him at His feet, weeping she began to shower His feet with her tears and to wipe (them) off with the hair of her head, and she kept kissing His feet hard and anointing them with myrrh." (vs. 38)

The first verb of vs. 38 is often translated "she stood behind Him at His feet" or "standing behind Him ..". Jesus was not seated in a chair, but was reclining at the table (vs. 36), so that His feet were off the floor. She, of course, was not allowed to take such a posture. Entering the room, she spotted Him, walked up to Him, and positioned herself behind Him at His feet. It is obvious that she could not keep kissing Him, if she had been standing. She must have been on her knees. Hence our translation: "Having taken her position." The verb is in the Aorist aspect. If she was standing all the time, the Present aspect would be more appropriate.

We would note that, with the exception of "began" all the remaining five verbs are in the Present aspect. She kept weeping, showering, wiping off, kissing, and anointing. Speaking to Simon, His host, Jesus highlights in a very explicit form one of the things she kept doing: "since I entered your house, she did not *stop* kissing my feet hard" (vs. 45). For the other four verbs Luke uses the Aorist aspect, though Jesus mentions the other four things she repeatedly did. Providing water for washing of feet, anointing, and kissing were all the standard routine of hospitality, which Jesus pointed out that his host had failed to observe. It is intriguing why Luke uses the Aorist aspect with the verb for kissing alone.

Earlier, in connection with Gn 22.6, 8, we touched on the question of repetition. In this story which is not particularly long the feet of Jesus are mentioned three times in vs. 38. In drawing the matter to Simon's attention, Jesus mentions His own feet four times. Didn't it suffice to use the noun only once and refer to it later with *them*, a pronoun? The repetition of the word appears to be deliberate. Jesus was touched and moved by what she had kept doing to His feet. In the West and the biblical world there is nothing special with guests being kissed or people kissing each other when they meet. Even then, however, the parts of your body to be kissed are lips, forehead, or hands, but feet are rarely kissed. Deeply conscious of her sinful past, the woman probably could not look Jesus in the face, and took her position at His feet. That is probably when she noticed that His feet were still covered with dust, and decided to clean them with her tears that kept pouring out of her eyes. The ointment she applied to His feet was probably no cheap stuff, but equivalent to perfume of Chanel, which she kept pouring out on His feet profusely.[4]

An average woman might hug Jesus, saying, "Lord Jesus, how glad I am to meet you!" One does not know how many minutes elapsed since she entered the room and left. It is remarkable that, during those minutes, she did not utter a single word. Nor did she say: "Lord, thank You so much. I respect you so much from the bottom of my heart!" Turning to Simon, Jesus said: "Let me say to you. From the love she has shown for Me you can see that her many sins are already forgiven. One who is forgiven little, loves little" (vs. 47). She must have been truly grateful to Him. Her emotions got over her and she couldn't say a word. Your love could be communicated non-verbally; you don't have to keep saying, "Oh, I love you, I love you."

Here I remember an anecdote told in a biography of William Booth, the founder of the Salvation Army. It was about a charming, pretty, and young Scottish missionary who had been sent to a rural village in India. She did not have much to show for her years' dedicated missionary efforts. One day a groaning Indian was brought to her. She saw a huge thorn in one of his feet, which they could not pull out. All she had was an emergency kit. She did not have a forceps which a medical practitioner would use in such a situation. All of a sudden she put her teeth round the thorn and pulled it out. The following day she was visited by the Indian accompanied by his family and friends. Then a good number of untouchables in the village, who are at the bottom of the hierarchical Indian society, began to be converted to the Christian faith and be baptised. Many of those new converts found her sermons not easy to follow. But for them, the white, beautiful, young Western woman putting her beautiful teeth to the dirtiest part of the Indian's leg counted far more than her oral message.

Shortly before being hung on the cross, Jesus had a supper with His closest disciples. During the meal He put a towel round His waist, poured water into a bucket, washed the feet of every disciple, and wiped them with the towel. The Bible says that Jesus loved them with an utmost love (Joh 13.1). He washed

---

[4] Shortly before His crucifixion, Jesus visited the home of Lazarus He had resurrected. When Martha was busy serving Him a meal, Mary poured a generous amount of precious perfume of nard on His feet, wiped them with her hair, and the room filled with the odour of the ointment (Joh 12.3). Though Mary may also have repeated her actions, the Greek verbs are all in the Aorist aspect. The expensive nature of the ointment used is highlighted, as it was picked up by Judas the Iscariot and criticised as a meaningless waste. Thus the focus in the two stories differs between them.

even the feet of Judas, who would shortly betray Him. As He did so, He may have been thinking of what that woman did for him at the Pharisee's.

In the above-quoted "Let me say to you. From the love she has shown for Me you can see that her many sins are already forgiven. One who is forgiven little, loves little" (vs. 47) the Greek verb "are forgiven" is in the Perfect aspect. The forgiveness had already taken place prior to Jesus's statement to Simon. At her departure He repeated the same statement to her and added: "Your faith has saved you" (vs. 50), again the Perfect aspect. Jesus could not possibly be contradicting St Paul on this fundamental issue of salvation. Paul was very firm in his teaching: we can be saved only with belief in Jesus Christ and His gracious self-sacrifice, and never through our own good deeds. On arrival at Simon the Pharisee's this woman had already believed in Jesus. She used to be treated as a hopeless case. However, when she heard of Jesus or saw His deeds and how He related to sinners, a ray of hope had started shining on her, and she became desirous of seeing Him personally, who had helped her to decide to part with her past way of life. On her arrival, as far as Jesus was concerned, her salvation was a fait accompli. We thus learn that the selection of the two central verbs in the Perfect aspect carries such a profound meaning.

In stressing the importance of the bodily resurrection of Jesus the apostle writes: "Christ died for our sins according to the scriptures and He was buried, and He has been resurrected on the third day according to the scriptures, and He appeared to Cephas, then to the twelve" (1Cor 15.3-5). Of the four Greek verbs used here only that concerning His resurrection is in the Perfect aspect, the remainder in the Aorist aspect. When two women came to Jesus' grave, they were told by an angel: "He is not here. He was resurrected" (Lk 24.6), some of His disciples said: "the Lord was indeed resurrected, and appeared to Simon" (vs. 34). In both cases the same verb is used, but in the Aorist aspect. Jesus' virgin birth, crucifixion, burial, and resurrection have been the essential components of the Gospel message (ké:rygma), as confessed in the Apostolic Creed. For Paul, however, Jesus' death, burial and post-resurrection appearances are not merely objective, historical facts. After having appeared to the disciples who were miles ahead of him in terms of the belief in Christ, He appeared to him as well, one who was convinced that this new belief, "Jesus religion," ought to be demolished, and was accordingly busy doing his best to this end, appeared to Paul in a very special, unique way on the way to Damascus, and found it right to speak to him personally (Acts 9.1-6). That event meant to Paul much more than a mere historical fact. Years on, as he was writing to the church in Corinth, he thought that that voice of the resurrected Jesus still kept ringing in his ears. Such a perception of that unique event cannot be expressed better than in the Perfect aspect.

A couple of summers ago I attended a European Japanese Christian retreat held in Leipzig, and read Luther's 95 theses. The first reads, translated into English: "When our Lord Jesus Christ said, 'Repent,' He meant to say that his believers' life on earth should be a constant penance." He is citing Mt 4.17. I thought that the conclusion Luther had drawn from this New Testament passage was rather striking, and wondered how he had come to it. When I opened the Scripture in the Greek original, I discovered for the first time that the imperative, "Repent," is in the Present aspect. This command was given shortly after He Himself had been baptised by John. Luther wanted to say that our repentance must be much more than a confession of our past sins which we make at the time of our baptism in the presence of the congregation of the church you are about to join. Every time we realise that we have gone wrong, we need to repent of our sins and ask for God's forgiveness.

One evening, when Jesus and His disciples were crossing the Lake Galilee in a small boat, a violent squall began blowing. Jesus, dead tired from the day's work, was in deep sleep in the stern. When He was awaked by His scared disciples, He instantly acted and there was a great calm. He used two imperative forms; the first in the Present aspect, 'Remain quiet,' and the second in the Perfect aspect of a verb meaning 'to muzzle an animal to prevent it from going for grass when it should be working' (Mk 4.39). There must have been a deafening noise. With the first imperative, He said to the wind: "Stop making that noise." The Perfect aspect of the second imperative implies that the wind had already been muzzled. In colloquial English we might say: "Keep your mouth shut." Though impossible in English, Greek has imperative forms in the third person. Jesus could have used such with the wind or lake as their grammatical subject. But the forms are actually in the second person. He who was present at the creation of the universe could communicate with the elements in Hebrew or Aramaic. Mark uses this second verb elsewhere, though in the Aorist aspect this time. When Jesus and His disciples were worshipping in a synagogue in Capernaum, a man in a serious psychiatric condition started talking to Him, and He scolded the overpowering demon with "Shut up and get out" (Mk 1.25); the second verb must mean "to get out of the miserable demoniac," not "out of the synagogue."

Let us take a look at a couple of examples from the Septuagint.

When Uriah died, Joab sent a report to David from the frontline, making sure that the herald concluded the report with "your servant Uriah the Hittite also died" (2Sm 11.21). See above at p. 41. The Old Greek uses here the verb in the Perfect aspect, whereas in exactly the same Hebrew sentence as told by the narrator himself the Aorist aspect is used (vs. 17). Joab wanted to reassure his boss: "Uriah has died. Your nightmare is over, sir." In describing what the herald actually said, Uriah's death is reported in the Perfect aspect, but in the same breath mention is made of other casualties among David's troops, for which the Aorist aspect has been selected. We see here a commendable, skilful use by the Old Greek translator of the resources available in Greek.

In commanding his subordinate as to how to go about slaying Amnon, who had humiliated his dear sister, Absalom said: "When Amnon begins to feel good with wine, I shall say to you: 'Attack Amnon and kill him!' Don't be scared" (2Sm 13.28). The Old Greek uses the imperative "Don't be scared" in the Present aspect. Absalom may have noticed that some of his soldiers were already visibly scared, shuddering. In a similar context we find an imperative in the Aorist aspect, e.g. "Don't fear, don't lose heart (never)" (Josh 8.1) and "Don't fear them (never)" (10.8), in both cases God speaking to Joshua. The New Testament offers a more illuminating example. As Jesus was about to send out the just appointed twelve apostles into the rough and threatening world, He told them not to fear opponents as many as three times in the course of a mere four verses, and Matthew uses one and the same Greek verb, /fobéomai/. However, on the first occasion the imperative is in the Aorist aspect (Mt 10.26), when He was telling the apostles what their general mindset and attitude should be. When He started elaborating actual, scary situations which might confront them, the imperative shifts to the Present aspect (vs. 28 and 31). Matthew may be wanting to say that Jesus noticed some apostles now looking scared and beginning to shake.[5]

---

[5] When an English classicist was learning Modern Greek, he was puzzled by his teacher, a Greek, who would shout at a dog barking beside him "Don't bark!" by using the imperative in the Present aspect. One day, whilst reading Plato's *Apology of Socrates*, he noted that, when Socrates, speaking in a court, says "Gentlemen, please do not get agitated over these matters!" by using the imperative in the Aorist aspect in a preliminary warning, but shifts to the Present aspect, when Socrates sees some agitation going on among the audience.

A story is told of a French classicist. He went to Greece to work on an archaeological site. When he wanted to take a close look at an excavated stone tablet with an inscription engraved on it, he asked a hired, local Greek labourer to turn it over. The Greek kept turning the tablet over. The erudite French scholar must have wrongly used the imperative in the Present aspect.

Chapter III

Aramaic

Some people might say, "Well, I know a thing or two about Hebrew and Greek. But, Aramaic? What is it?" Though only a tiny portion of the Bible is written in it, those who insist on translating the Bible from its original languages need to know it. The Aramaic portions are all in the Old Testament: Ezr 4.8-6.18, 7.12-26, Dan 2.4b-7.28, Jer 10.11. The Aramaic section of the book of Daniel bears great theological significance. The history of this language can fairly compete with that of Hebrew. The oldest Aramaic document currently known is thought to date from the ninth century BCE. Among ancient languages still in use Aramaic is thus probably superseded by Chinese alone. In late 1979 a statue with an inscription engraved on both of its sides was discovered in Tell el-Fekheriye in a North-eastern corner of Syria. It is dedicated to a local leader and written bilingually in Assyrian, the official language of the Assyrian Empire, and Aramaic, a common language of the ruled local population. It is agreed to date to 850 BCE at the latest. The status of Aramaic as a cross-cultural lingua franca equivalent to the status enjoyed nowadays by English would remain in place for centuries to come in the Ancient Near East. Against this background we can understand a desperate request put by Hezekiah's courtiers to a commander of the Assyrian army, Rabshakeh, who, most likely through an interpreter, did his best to demonstrate, in Hebrew, the folly of being hooked up on their present king and hoping for help by Egypt, and demanded a peaceful surrender (2Kg 18.26). They were fearful that the threatening message transmitted in the vernacular could upset the common folk besieged behind the walls. Hence, "Please do address us in Aramaic, an international, diplomatic language we are perfectly comfortable with, but Greek to the general populace." This happened in the year 701 BCE. In a later period, when King Nebuchadnezzar made a large number of Israelites move to Babylon, the exiles learned the local vernacular, Aramaic. This linguistic milieu is reflected in stories told in the book of Daniel, a book which, in its present form, was finalised only in the first half of the second century BCE, centuries after the events depicted in its Aramaic chapters. The Babylonian Empire was followed by the Persian. Although Persian and Aramaic were miles apart from each other, the Persian leadership found it not only convenient, but geopolitically sensible and advantageous to adopt Aramaic as its official language, for it had already become a common means of communication not only in the Near East, but also in Kandahar in South East Afghanistan. Stories told in the book of Ezra as played out on such a stage of the Persian Empire were most realistically composed in Aramaic. The penetration of Aramaic among the Jewish community, not only in its diasporas, but also in their native Holy Land, only grew firmer with the passage of time, though it would never totally dislodge Hebrew. Among the Dead Sea Scrolls we find Aramaic documents which were, until their discovery, known only in a later translation such as *Enoch* and *Tobit*, but also a document which was unknown beforehand such as *The Genesis Apocryphon* and Aramaic translations of Old Testament books such as *Job* and a fragment of *Leviticus*. That Jesus gripped a hand of s synagogue leader's dead daughter and addressed her /tali<u>th</u>á qum/ 'Girl, get up!' in Aramaic (Mk 5.41) proves that not only Jesus, but also the girl were comfortable in Aramaic; here we are not about a simple greeting such as "Hello, how are you?," which many could say in more than one language other than their mother tongue. In His last agony and excruciating pain on the cross Jesus exclaimed partly in Aramaic: /elí elí lma <u>sh</u>vaqtáni/ 'my God, my God, why have You abandoned me?' (Mt 27.46).[1] Aramaic must have taken so deep roots in the community concerned. And yet the view which was almost universally accepted till about 1950 that, round the time of Jesus, Hebrew had ceased to be spoken and had become a language of prayer intelligible only to the intellectual and religious elite among the Jewish community has now been laid to rest. The vast quantity of Hebrew documents of diverse literary types, *genres*, originating from 11 caves on the northern shore of the Dead Sea and the Judaean Desert nearby that began to appear since 1947 has proved indisputably that, at least till the beginning of the second century CE, Hebrew was far from dead, but very much kicking. These Hebrew documents contain not only copies of Old Testament books, but non-biblical books, the vast majority of which were unknown before. There are also indications that Hebrew was still being spoken, maybe not by everybody and everywhere. However, when the last resistance led by Bar Kokhba against the Roman rule collapsed in 135 CE, Hebrew breathed its last. Thereafter no Jew learned to speak it as his or her mother tongue until the rise of the political and cultural Zionism under the banner of Eliezer Ben

---

[1] The verb translated 'abandoned' can hardly be Hebrew. /lma/ 'why?' is also Aramaic. /elí/ 'my God' is Hebrew.

Yehuda and others. A modern Israeli author once lamented, though with a grain of humour: "our country is where parents learn their mother tongue from their children." Children of immigrants were picking up the new language faster than their parents.

Syriac, a post-Christian dialect of Aramaic, would eventually reach the Far East. In 1625 a bi-lingual (Syriac - Chinese) stele built in 781 in Sian in North China was discovered, testifying to the evangelising work by Nestorian missionaries there.

Franz Rosenthal, an eminent scholar of Yale University, once stated: "... the history of Aramaic represents the purest triumph of the human spirit as embodied in language (which is the mind's most direct form of physical expression) over the crude displays of material power .... Great empires were conquered by the Aramaic language, and when they disappeared and were submerged in the flow of history, that language persisted and continued to live a life of its own." Thus Aramaic speaking worlds conquered the world, without becoming a political, military force and establishing an empire.

Given this survey on Aramaic, it should be obvious that some familiarity with it could throw interesting light on our understanding not only of the Old Testament, but also the New. Given the multilingual milieu of the Holy Land in the first century CE, it is no wonder that some New Testament writers should have inserted Aramaic words and expressions which were current in their time. Apart from /talitá qum/ and /shvaqtáni/ mentioned earlier, /aqél damá/ 'the field of blood' (Acts 1.19), /ke:fá:s/ 'rock' (Joh 1.42), /tabithá:/ 'gazelle' (Acts 9.36), /abbá/ 'father' (Ro 8.15), /marána tha/ 'our Lord, come!' (1Cor 16.22) come to one's mind. Both Hebrew and Aramaic are written with the same alphabet. There are plenty of similarities in grammar and vocabulary, too. For instance, 'a good king' is /mélekh tov/ in Hebrew, /mélekh tav/ in Aramaic. Those who know one of the two languages reasonably well would have little difficulty in learning the other.

A) Singular and plural

Just like English, all the three biblical languages distinguish between singular and plural. This applies not only to nouns, but also to pronouns, adjectives, and verbs. Hence the ambiguity inherent in English as in 'you went' is alien to those languages. The form chosen for *you* indicates whether you were solitary or one of a group. If you are going to mention *book*, you need to know in advance its quantity before you open your mouth or start pressing keys.

This number distinction, however, is not universal. There are languages in the world which have only one form of any noun as Chinese, Korean, and Japanese.[2] Native speakers of these languages are annoyed when learning English, for instance: they need to learn that the same ending spelled with the same letter sounds different when attached to *book* and *size*, and a host of other irregularities, e.g. *man*, but *men*. Some years ago, when I taught Beginners' Hebrew in Shanghai, I said to my students: "you may have heard from your English teacher from England or America that English is very logical, for you can say *one book*, but only *three books*. But when you add *three*, what is really illogical with *three book*?".

The first of the Ten Commandments makes it absolutely clear that polytheism is an anathema (Ex 20.3-4). However, we encounter a striking phenomenon in Hebrew. It has two nouns for 'god.' Though they sound somewhat similar, they are two distinct words: /el/ and /elóah/. The first was used by Jesus on the cross with /-i/ 'my' added as cited above, /elí elí/. It is also known from /immánuel/ 'God with us' Is 7.14. /el/ occurs in the Old Testament 235 times and /elóah/ 2,570 times. Both denote a transcendental, super-human being, thus safely translatable with 'god.' Both are occasionally used with reference to a pagan deity or deities, but mostly refer to the monotheistic god of the Bible. The most striking thing here is that, when /elóah/ refers to the only god, it is used in the singular a mere 53 times, whilst in the overwhelming majority of cases it is used in the plural. Even then, however, when the word serves as the grammatical subject of a verb, the latter appears in the singular. Even in the famous pronouncement, "Hear, o Israel, Yahweh our God is one" (Dt 6.4) the plural form, /elohím/, is used.

By contrast, the two other biblical languages, Aramaic and Greek, are absolutely 'logical.' When Jesus was asked by a naughty scribe "Which of the commandments is the most important?," He answered "You shall love your God with all your heart, and with all your soul, and with all your mind" (Mt 22.36-37). If the exchange had taken place in Hebrew, Jesus would have used the plural form of /elóah/, but the Greek text here uses the singular form and the definite article is added. There is no doubt whatsoever as to what Jesus meant. However, if the language of this exchange were Aramaic, a sister language of Hebrew and so close to it, He would have used the singular form. Should He,

---

[2] Japanese, for instance, can express *mountains* differently than *mountain* by repeating the word in question: /yama/ as against /yama yama/. This, however, occurs with a small number of nouns only. Nor is the repetition obligatory, if two speakers are gazing at a mountain range and admiring their majesty. To say *three mountains* one never repeats /yama/.

for Heaven's sake, have erred, the scribe, shaking his head, might have asked Him: "Really? Gods of which people are you referring to, please?".

In the Aramaic passages of the book of Daniel the singular form is used when Daniel speaks of the God he is serving, whilst he uses the plural, when referring to gods of Babylonians in whose midst he lives. E.g. "you have praised the gods of silver and gold …, which do not see nor hear nor understand, but the God in whose hand is your life and who determine your paths you have not praised" (Dan 5.23). That is how Daniel reminds Belshazzar of his error. When challenged by Nebuchadnezzar with "Is it true that you do not serve my gods nor worship the golden image which I have set up?" (Dan 3.14), Daniel's three colleagues, without mincing words, throw his challenge to the wind: "Are you questioning if the God we serve is really capable of rescuing us? He can, o king, rescue us out of the burning furnace and out of your hand. But if not, be it known to you, o King, that we are not going to serve your gods nor worship the golden image that you have set up" (vs. 17-18). Subsequently, as he was gazing into the furnace, the king remarks: "the fourth looks like a son of gods" (vs. 25). At that point his mindset was still that of the polytheistic world familiar to him and accordingly worded his impression of the rescuer who looked different from an ordinary human being. Shortly afterwards, however, he makes a confession as a born-again monotheist: "Praised be the god of Shadrach, Meshach, and Abednego, who sent his angel and rescued his servants who trusted in him and acted against the king's decree and gave up their bodies in order not to serve nor worship any god other than their god" (vs. 28), where their god is consistently being referred to in the singular — god, his, him. The king, using the same title, "the exalted god," which Daniel uses, speaking to Belshazzar, the king's successor (Dan 5.18), circulates his view and shares his marvellous experiences throughout the empire: "it pleases me to make you known the signs and marvels which he wrought towards me. How great are his signs and how powerful his marvels are! His kingdom is an eternal kingdom and his reign is for generations to come" (Dan 3.32-33). Daniel and his colleagues must have used the plural form for god when they talked in Hebrew among themselves, but in their conversation in Aramaic with the king and locals, they must have taken care in order that their Aramaic is not wrongly influenced by Hebrew. Exactly like their distant forefather, Joseph, they had made a very impressive achievement in the foreign land. All the same it must have been quite a challenge and effort in their subordinate status to hold fast to their ancestral faith. They put their lives on the line, and that pleased their God, and their witness helped the local leadership have their eyes opened to a totally new outlook.

The use in Hebrew of the plural form of the word for god is one of a small number of exceptions. Most of the time the line between singular and plural is clearly drawn. Hence, most translations are wrong with their *at night* or *by night* at Ps 134.1, where the noun for *night* is in the plural. So translate: "Bless the Lord, all the servants of the Lord, who minister in the Lord's house night after night."

B) Language and culture

Any language is an important ingredient of the culture of its speech community. Not only can we talk about and discuss a culture with the medium of a language, but the language itself often reflects the society, culture, mode of thinking, and world view of its speakers. In that sense, studying a foreign language introduces its students to a new world and broadens their cultural horizon. Common words such as *brother* and *sister* in English have each two distinct words in Chinese, Japanese, and Korean. When translating an English text, you come across *my brother* applied to someone for the first time in the text, you would have to put a question mark above. When you read on and discover in the sequel who is older, *I* or *my brother*, you can now select the right word for *brother*. This is due to the Confucian ethics that has influenced the mode of thinking of speakers of these three East Asian languages.

A little over twenty years ago I took part in a project of translating the Bible into Japanese. One of the books that was assigned to me was Daniel. The editorial committee, on noticing my use of the word *sáke* to render /yáyin/, a word which is rendered in English with *wine*, pointed out to me that Japanese has a composite word that is translatable as 'grape sake.'[3] This Hebrew word is etymologically related to /óinos/ in Greek (/wóinos/ in an earlier period), an indication that the alcoholic drink made from grapes has its origin in the Mediterranean world: *wine*, *Wein* (German), *vin* (French) all go back to these ancient words. In Japan, the transliterated form /wáin/ is used and the product is drunk, though the average Japanese cannot afford it; it is not native, but imported from overseas. In France, one can hardly think of a meal without wine, even in working-class families. I doubt that Nebuchadnezzar got drunk from an imported vodka, but from a local product. *sáke* is its precise equivalent in the Japanese society. Interestingly the Chinese Bible also uses the same character as for *sáke* in translating the Hebrew and Aramaic words in question. At the end the editorial committee let me off the hook.

---

[3] I used /sáke/ also to translate the Aramaic word /chamár/, also meaning 'wine.'

I would like to discuss here another matter which also belongs to the vocabulary of secular, material culture. At the start of His public ministry Jesus fasted in the wilderness of Judaea forty days and forty nights. He probably refrained from wine as well. Then the devil challenged Him: "If you are the son of God, command these stones to become bread" (Mt 4.3). Jesus' answer is one of the best known verses of the Bible. He quotes from the Old Testament: "Man shall not live by bread alone" (Dt 8.3). Every Japanese Bible, whether archaic or contemporary, uses here a loan word, /pan/, a transliteration of *pain* in French. In Japan the recent decades have witnessed a dramatic increase in the consumption of bread. My daily breakfast has been one and a half pieces of toasted bread smeared with some fruit jam and a cup of coffee for donkey's years. My wife knows, however, that cooked rice, /góhan/, is the principal ingredient for my lunch and supper. Strangely, however, Japanese Bibles use /káte/ 'food' in another famous verse, "Give us this day our daily bread" (Mt 6.11). Both at Mt 4.3 and 6.11 the Chinese Bible uses a word meaning 'food.' In the Western and Middle Eastern culture the word meaning 'bread' is used not only in its literal sense, but also as a generic expression of life-sustaining food, as shown by the English expression, *bread-winner*. Then /góhan/ appears to me to be the best Japanese translation in these two Matthaean passages. I read somewhere that, at the end of the 19th century, European and American missionaries celebrated the eucharist or the Lord's Supper with Japanese converts by sharing small rice-balls and /sáke/. The Chinese character used to indicate bread at Mt 26.26, where Jesus is depicted as instituting the eucharist, is one that is used in Japanese for 'flat rice cake.'[4]

C) Jerusalem

The name of the holy city is known as *Jerusalem*. This *e* as the last vowel, however, is an Aramaic way of pronouncing the name as in the Aramaic sections of the books of Daniel and Ezra. Its Hebrew pronunciation is /yrushaláyim/. If we ignore the vowel signs added to the Hebrew text in the post-Christian era, there is no way the end of the name can be pronounced /-áyim/. For this impossible pronunciation we would need another letter between the last two: /l - y - m/. The city is mentioned 641 times in the Hebrew Bible, and only five times, all in late books such as Chronicles, Esther, and Jeremiah, it is spelled with this

---

[4] Dr George K.W. Mak of Hong Kong Baptist University informs me that this character is used in all the extant Chinese translations of the Bible.

extra consonant, /y/. In Dead Sea scrolls the longer form is more common. In a text dating to the 14 century BCE and written by a foreigner we see /urusalim/. It is interesting that Biblical Aramaic, which is several centuries later than Biblical Hebrew, preserved the more archaic pronunciation of this important place-name.

CHAPTER IV

SEPTUAGINT AS A BRIDGE BETWEEN THE OLD AND THE NEW TESTAMENTS

My M.A. thesis written in Tokyo under the supervision of the late Prof. Masao Sekine was a study trying to show how a monosyllabic word, /ho:s/, of extremely high frequency, is used in the Greek Bible. The Greek Bible is comprised of the New Testament, which is wholly in Greek, and Septuagint, an ancient, pre-Christian Greek translation of the entire Old Testament. As a matter of fact, Septuagint incorporates other pre-Christian documents, which traditionally go under the name of 'Apocrypha' and 'Pseudepigrapha,' and includes books such as *Maccabees* and *Sirach* or *Ecclesiasticus*. For the sake of comparison I also investigated the use of this Greek word in other contemporary Greek documents.

Over 33 years I taught at three universities outside of Japan. Though I was appointed to teach and research Semitic languages, my interest in Greek was with me all the time, and I occupied myself with it on the side. Some might wonder if a research on how the German of Goethe is translated into English constitutes a worthwhile object of scientific research. On the following pages I shall do my best to demonstrate that the Septuagint does indeed merit scientific attention, and it is enlightening in many a way. The International Organization for Septuagint and Cognate Studies established more than half a century ago boasts of nearly 800 members, holds an international meeting every three years and meets regionally in between, and publishes an annual. Since my retirement in 2003 I have been able to devote much research time not only to Semitic languages, but also to the Septuagint. Ten years ago I had my *A Greek-English Lexicon of the Septuagint* (Peeters: Leuven), a book of about 800 pages in the A-4 format, published. Two years ago *A Syntax of Septuagint Greek* (Peeters: Leuven), nearly 1,000 pages also in the A-4 format, saw the light of day. More than one reason can be mentioned as to why I am so deeply involved in Septuagint research. One important reason is that this document represents an important bridge between the two Testaments. As a consequence of the successful

campaign of Hellenisation launched by Alexander the Great Greek became an
international language in the Mediterranean world, Northern Africa, the Near
East, and even Pakistan. At home and in exchanges among locals alone traditional, local languages reigned supreme, whereas those who had dealings with
foreigners found the reasonable command of Greek a practical necessity, just
like English these days. When St Paul started his missionary work outside of
the Holy Land, he would first seek contact with local Jewish communities.
Members of such a community, with the possible exception of new arrivals from
the Holy Land, those who had been there tens of years or the second or third
generation would have had serious trouble with Hebrew and Aramaic, and such
people would have been much more comfortable in Greek except those belong-
ing to the local, religious elite. It is generally thought that, in the first half of
the third century BCE, the translation of the Old Testament into Greek was
undertaken to meet this crying need, though there were more motives for such
an undertaking. It was natural that they had tackled the Pentateuch first, soon
followed by the remainder of the Old Testament canon. Beside the above-mentioned apocryphal documents, other documents originally composed in Greek
such as 3 and 4 Maccabees would subsequently be incorporated, making the
final product quite a voluminous one, more voluminous than the Old and New
Testaments put together. What one is to bear in mind here is that, prior to the
advent of Jesus Christ, the Septuagint must have deeply penetrated the Jewish
society and the majority of overseas Jews read their Old Testament in Greek.
Gentiles who came into contact with those Jews and became proselytes and later
Christians would no doubt have read the Greek Old Testament. This holds also
for gentiles who heard the Gospel through St Paul and were converted to the
Christian faith. Then, when St Paul says "Every scripture is inspired by God
and is beneficial to teaching etc." (2Tim 3.16), he must have meant the Old
Testament text read by Timothy and all readers of this epistle in this Septuagint
version.

It also follows that members of early churches read the Old Testament in the
Septuagint. So did many New Testament writers. Though Greek had become a
global language, the uneducated masses needed a Bible in their mother tongue.
Thus the Septuagint was done into Coptic, Ethiopic, Armenian, Georgian, Arabic, and so on. Familiarity with, and good knowledge of, the Septuagint could
enhance our understanding of the Greek language of the New Testament.
I would also add that the matter is not concerned with the Greek grammar and
vocabulary alone. Translation, whether oral or in writing, presupposes an interpreter's or translator's understanding of what he hears or reads in the foreign
language concerned. The Septuagint, then, could be said to be the oldest

commentary on the Old Testament. Below we shall look at some concrete examples.[1]

A) "In the beginning God made heaven and earth" (Gn 1.1)

I happen to know of no translation other than the Septuagint that translates the first verse of the Bible by using a common verb denoting 'to make.' St Jerome, in his Latin translation, says *creavit*. Theologians speak of *creatio ex nihilo*, 'creation out of nothing.' The Hebrew verb used here, /bará/, occurs in Biblical Hebrew more than 50 times. Ignorance of such a common word would have disqualified the translator right 'in the beginning.' Our translator, however, writes "May Abraham be blessed by the most High God, the creator of heaven and earth" (Gn 14.19), where the Hebrew text uses a very common verb /qaná/ 'to make.' He apparently wants to underline the opposition between maker and made.

B) Love comes in more than one form

Some of you no doubt have heard or read that Greek has three words denoting love: nouns — /éro:s/, /filía/, /agápe:/ and the corresponding verbs — /eráo:/, /filéo:/, /agapáo:/. This matter has been intensively studied in the past, so much so that a small bookshelf might not be able to hold all books, journal articles, and encyclopaedia entries written and published on the subject. The first pair, roughly speaking, concerns love between humans, often between two genders, though, contrary to its derivative, *erotic*, does not necessarily imply sex acts. It occurs, however, only a few times in the Septuagint, and not at all in the New Testament. So we shall concentrate here on the last two pairs. /filía/ is said to be love between friends, whereas /agápe:/ relates not only to friends in the narrow sense, but also is said to derive from respect and care towards other people, and in that sense superior to /filía/. Paul mentions as virtues essential to Christians "faith, hope, love" (1Cor 13.13), and accords the highest priority to love, for which he uses the word /agápe:/. When Christian believers are admonished to love one another, the verb used is /agapáo:/. So Joh 15.12, 17, Ro 13.8. At Joh 13.14 this mutual love (/agápe:/) was introduced by Jesus as a new

---

[1] In this introductory section the definite article has been added, so *the* Septuagint. However, it is known that the first, pre-Christian translation would subsequently undergo revision in various stages. See above at p. 36, f.n. 3.

commandment as against the old of the Old Testament. In commending mutual love Jesus advises His disciples to seek a model in His love towards them: 'as I loved you' (Joh 15.12 /agapáo:/). St Paul exhorts: "Husbands, love your wives, as also Jesus loved the church and gave Himself up for her" (Eph 5.25 /agapáo:/).[2] We see that God's love for the humankind is the best model of /agápe:/. This is not a teaching unique to the New Testament. God called Abraham 'my beloved' (Is 41.8, 2Ch 20.7, LXX[3] /agapáo:/). Even earlier, Moses told his coreligionists that it was because of God's love of Abraham and their descendants that He had led the children of Israel out of their slavery in Egypt to the promised land (Dt 4.37, LXX /agapáo:/).

On the other hand, Jesus called His close disciples friends (/fílos/) (Joh 15.15). So also "If you practise what I command you, then you are My friends" (vs. 14). Furthermore, He mentioned /fílos/ and /agápe:/ in one breath: "there is no greater love (/agápe:/) than someone sacrificing his life for the sake of his friends (/fílos/)" (vs. 13). This shows that the two notions are not mutually exclusive, but complement each other. The selection of the plural form (/fíloi/) here is hinting at Jesus' crucifixion.

The verb /fíleo:/ is sometimes used in the sense of 'to kiss' as an expression of affection. By contrast, /agapáo:/ is never so used. This, however, does not have to mean that the latter is about a superior love, Platonic love as against erotic love. /agapáo:/ is used of a man madly falling in love with a woman as in "the extra seven years Jacob slaved for Rachel's father looked so short in his eyes, because he was so much in love (/agapáo:/) with her" (Gn 29.20). The same is true of a love-song sung by a young couple (Ct 3.2-4). This verb is also applied to a geisha's customers or lovers (Ezk 16.37).

There is an important difference between the two Greek verbs under discussion here. /fíleo:/ is something that arises in your heart naturally and by itself. Hence it is hardly ever used in the imperative. By contrast, as shown in some of the examples quoted above, /agapáo:/ can be something you are commanded to do. Jesus taught: "Love your enemies and pray for those who persecute you" (Mt 5.44), something that goes against your inborn grain, something that we can and should strive to practise by relying on One who gave up His life for us. As noted above, Jesus introduced mutual love as a new *commandment*, and we shall see below (pp. 92f.) that He summed up the entire biblical ethics under two *commandments* of the love for God and the love for neighbours. It is interesting

---

[2] Here the apostle is not speaking of mutual love, for he exhorts wives to obey their husbands (vs. 22).

[3] LXX = Septuagint.

to note that /filéo:/ in the sense of 'to kiss' *is* used in the imperative twice in the Septuagint (Gn 27.26; Ct 1.2).

Here is another important matter: Biblical Hebrew has virtually only one word that denotes love. One may love God, neighbours, pets, tangible objects or intangible ideas, e.g. food (Gn 27.4), wine (Pr 21.17), money (Ec 5.9), wisdom (Pr 29.3), righteousness (Is 61.8), longevity (Ps 34.13), idle slumber (Pr 20.13), and so on.

This imbalance between Hebrew and Greek makes interesting the Septuagint rendition of Jacob's attitude towards Joseph born from his favourite wife, Rachel, and his brothers as described at the start of Gn 37. The Hebrew text may be rendered as "And Israel loved Joseph best of all his sons, because he was a son born to him in his old age, and he had a multicoloured tunic made for him. And his brothers noticed that their father loved him better than all his brothers, and they hated him and could not speak to him calmly" (vs. 3-4). The Hebrew text uses here one and the same verb, /aháv/, for 'loved' twice over with the same subject (Israel) and object (Joseph). The Septuagint, however, varies the translation: /agápao:/ in vs. 3, but /filéo:/ in vs. 4. Another interesting detail here is the use of two distinct verbs in Vulgata, the Latin translation completed by Jerome (347-420), a renowned theologian and biblical scholar. He was dissatisfied with the then current Latin Bible, which had been translated from the Septuagint. He saw the need of a new translation based squarely on Hebrew and Aramaic. For this purpose he went to the Holy Land, settling in Bethlehem to receive instruction from local rabbis. His fundamental philosophy of this translation project was *Hebraica veritas*, 'Hebrew truth.' His selection of two verbs to render /aháv/ here is therefore all the more striking. Both Jerome and the Septuagint translator may have observed that vs. 4 is written from the perspective of Joseph's brothers. Jerome's selection of the passive voice accords nicely with this perspective: "when his brothers saw that he was loved better than all his brothers."

Our two Greek verbs are used in a dialogue conducted between Jesus and Peter on the shore of the Lake Galilee after Jesus' resurrection. Jesus asked: "Do you love (/agápao:/) me more than these people (do)?," to which Peter answered "Yes, sir, You know that I love (/filéo:/) You" (Joh 21.15). Exactly the same exchange took place once more (vs. 16). In vs. 17, however, we read "Peter became sad, because He said the third time 'Do you love (/filéo:/) me?'." Jesus did not ask the same question three times. It is remarkable that Jerome should use here also two Latin verbs, which are the same as in Gn 37, and moreover the two verbs used in the Septuagint at Gn 37 match those here: /agápao:/ = /dilígo/ and /filéo:/ = /ámo/. This is hardly arbitrary and whimsical on Jerome's part. Some New Testament scholars hold that John did not mean any semantic difference, but just changed the verbs for the sake of variety, thinking maybe that to repeat one verb six times over in such a proximity might look too crude and not imaginative enough. But I think otherwise. Just before His arrest in the garden of Gethsemane, after a meal with His disciples, He foretold them that they would all fall away when they witnessed what was going to happen to Him. Peter, however, was adamant that, even if these friends did fall away, and even if he had to die with Him, he would never ever say that he had nothing to do with Him. But when the verdict of death by crucifixion was announced, Peter emphatically declared that He was a total stranger to him. Here Jesus was seeking to find out where Peter now stood. He was probably hinting at what He had said to His disciples some time before: "there is no greater love (/agápe:/) than someone sacrificing his life for the sake of his friends (/fílos/)" (Joh 15.13). "Are you more than a friend to Me? Are you now willing to sacrifice your life for Me?" Jesus and Peter were speaking in Hebrew or Aramaic. It is not for nothing that an Aramaic dialect still being spoken today in Lebanon by a group of Christians, who are descendants of Jewish migrants from Galilee, has two distinct verbs for 'to love.'

C) Biblical love as understood by a 19th century Japanese politician cum soldier

The region of Japan, where I grew up, produced an outstanding politician cum soldier by the name of Takamori Saigo (1828-77). His motto of life was summarised in a brief statement written with four Chinese characters.[4] Its character by character English translation is "Revere heaven, love humans." After his death a copy of the Bible in Chinese was found in his private library. As one who was very close to the Imperial house and fought for the restoration he would have considered it indiscreet to say in public that he read the Bible.

One day, when Jesus was asked by a contemporary Bible scholar which was the most important commandment in the Bible, He answered: "Love the Lord your God with all your heart and with all your soul and with all your thought. This is the most important and first law. The second is similar to it. Love your neighbour as being like you. On these two commandments depend the law and the prophets" (Mt 22.36-40). It is unlikely that this teaching of Jesus should

---

[4] 敬天愛人.

escape Saigo's eyes. How one ought to live, one's *Lebensphilosophie*, taught in the thick Bible, has been reduced to these two principles. Jesus' audience would have noticed that He was quoting from Dt 6.5 and Lv 19.18. In Lk 10.25-28 Jesus, when asked "What should I do to inherit eternal life?", asked back "What is written in the Bible? You know, don't you?" When the same answer came back, Jesus gave him the full marks. Let us note, however, that the Old Testament itself does not mention these two commandments as summing up the most important two, and they occur in two separate books. This is then Jesus' own reading of the Bible and He also determined which is the first and which is the second. It is remarkable that Saigo summed these two sentences up with four Chinese characters.

These two most important commandments both use one and the same verb, 'to love.' That is the case in the Hebrew original and in the Chinese Bible. As an Oriental, however, Saigo may have been uneasy with the notion of 'to *love* God.' Educated in the classical Chinese literature and philosophy he knew that the transcendental being is referred to as 'heaven.'[5] Once he opted for *heaven*, the more appropriate verb to go with it was 'to *revere*' or 'to *hold in respect*.'

We looked at the story of the sinful woman meeting Jesus at Simon the Pharisee's (pp. 73ff.). In order to correct Simon's view on her, Jesus told him a parable about two debtors, one with a debt of 50 denarii and the other owing 500 denarii. When their creditor saw that neither of them had a chance of repaying on time, he wrote the debt of both off. Jesus asked Simon which of the two would *love* the creditor better. It may be a subjective judgement on my part, but here, too, I am not quite comfortable with the idea of a debtor *loving* his creditor. I would rather think that both debtors, especially the one who had the debt of 500 denarii[6] written off, would be deeply impressed with the incredible generosity and loving concern displayed by the creditor and begin to respect him and strive to follow such a philosophy of life.

Moreover, this four-character motto of Saigo is registered in a forty-volume Chinese lexical encyclopaedia completed in 1716 in China. I have been informed[7] that Emperor Kangxi, under whose reign this encyclopaedia came into being, had a scroll with this four-character statement *and* a seven-character statement exhorting to love people as one loves oneself and inscribed by himself

[5] It is perhaps chance, but remarkable all the same that, also in Judaism, *heaven* is a substitute for *god*. Thus 'the kingdom of heaven' in Matthew is parallel to 'the kingdom of God' in the synoptic Gospels.

[6] One denarius is said to what the average day labourer can earn by working one whole day.

[7] By Mrs Dr Ying Zhang of East China Normal University in Shanghai.

hanging on the wall of his room. Another surprising detail is that he presented a board with the first, shorter statement inscribed to the Immaculate Conception Cathedral in Beijing. The local Catholic Church accepted the board with 'Revere Heaven,' and not 'Love God'![8]

Here then we have a fascinating case of the Near East meeting the Far East.

D) Wash feet

Under B) above (pp. 89f.) we noted that the Hebrew verb for 'to love' is, in Gn 37, translated in the Septuagint with two distinct verbs, /agapáo:/ and /filéo:/. There are, however, cases in which one and the same verb is used in two distinct forms, but sharing the basic meaning.

Late one hot summer afternoon, Abraham, who was having a nap outside of his tent, heard approaching footsteps. He saw three strangers standing nearby, hastened to them, and prostrated himself in front of them. Perhaps judging from the way they were dressed, he concluded that they were no mere passers-by and decided to offer them a meal. He said: "I shall have some water brought. Please wash your feet and have a rest under the tree here" (Gn 18.4). Probably on the same evening, two of the guests arrived at Abraham's nephew Lot's in Sodom. Apparently he also guessed that the two were no mere travellers passing by, and said: "Please come to my home, stay overnight, and wash your feet. Then you could get up early in the morning and journey on" (Gn 19.2). It was a standard custom for guests to wash their feet before walking indoors.[9] The Hebrew text for "wash your feet" is exactly identical in the two passages. But their Septuagint rendition differs, although the same verb, /nípto:/, is used. In the first case it is in the imperative, active voice, third person, plural, i.e. 'Let them [= my servants] wash,' whereas in the second the form is in the imperative, middle voice, second person, plural. The middle voice often indicates that one does

---

[8] I do not know whether Saigo's motto is a creation of his own or a quote from this Chinese lexicon or one of its source texts. It is to be noted in this context that in a Japanese book published after his death by his friends, who put together a total of 43 statements attributed to him and sundry questions and answers, there is found one which elaborates this brief motto along the lines followed by Emperor Kangxi.

[9] Simon the Pharisee was gently reminded by Jesus of his failure to offer water for his guest to wash His feet on His arrival (Lk 7.44). In the 1980's I travelled to Eastern Turkey to study an old Syriac manuscript deposited at a local monastery. When I arrived at a local pastor's who had kindly offered me accommodation in his house, he promptly brought a bucket of water, which reminded me that the custom that was current in Abraham's days was still being practised.

something to oneself, for one's own interest. English has only two voices, active and passive. The Greek middle voice can be sometimes expressed by using a reflexive pronoun ending in *-self* or *-selves*. E.g. *she washed <u>herself</u>* as against *she washed her baby*. Lot is saying to his guests: 'I shall have water brought, but wash your feet yourselves.' Because the general context is analogous here, the guests are the same, and the stories are found in two adjoining chapters, the selection of the middle voice must be deliberate. The translator, comparing the two stories, probably felt that Lot's manners left something to be desired. Unlike his uncle, Lot was not seated in front of his home, but at the entrance of the city. On spotting the two strangers, he got to his feet, but, unlike Abraham, didn't dash to welcome them. Abraham offered them "a humble meal," which, literally translated, is "a piece of bread." But he directed Sarah to bake cakes with the finest flour, then ran to the cattle shed, caught a calf with good, tender meat, directed the cook to cook it, and took the bread spread with butter and a can of fresh milk. He may already have taken an early supper, so he did not dine with them, but stood beside them to make sure that his servants served them the meal properly. Lot, too, may already have had his evening meal, but did not even make a gesture of offering them a meal. He said instead: "Have a good sleep. Your departure tomorrow is rather early."

A similar example of the Greek translator's sensitivity occurs elsewhere in the book of Genesis. The group headed by Terah left Ur of the Chaldeans, heading for Canaan. On reaching Haran in the east of present-day Turkey, they decided to settle there. Terah would die there. Abram (later Abraham), a son of his, was married with Sarai. They must have been married quite some time, but with no child born from Sarai. At the age of 75 Abram was instructed to head for their ultimate destination, Canaan, and he departed with Sarai and Lot, an orphan nephew. At their departure God promised Abram to make him a great nation (Gn 12.2). Whether God meant *great* quantitatively or qualitatively is not immediately apparent, but *nation* implies more than one descendant. Some time later, on their arrival at their destination, God says to Abram: "[15]All the land that you see I will give to you and your offspring forever. [16]I will make your offspring like the dust of the earth, so that if anyone could count the dust, then your offspring could be counted" (Gn 13.15-16). There was now no ambiguity. Yet they had no child to carry their family line on. The same promise would subsequently be repeated a few more times with slight variations in wording. The situation must have been hard to take for Abram, who must have built up a solid position in the society. In the pre-modern Japan it was said of women: "Married three years and no child, then you leave." There is no trace of such a harsh regime in the Bible. Even so, many centuries later, one of their distinguished descendants would say: "Women complete their life's mission through child birth" (1Tim 2.15), so it must be even harder for Sarai to remain barren, looked down in the society. As she watched much younger women breast-feeding their babies happily, she must have sunken into the bottom of sorrow. One wouldn't blame her if she were bitter against God, who was supposed to have deliberately created mankind male and female, ensuring the conception for Eve's descendants; note what she said to her husband — "Look now, the Lord has prevented me from bearing children" (Gn 16.2). Not having experienced even any still birth, she had nearly resigned to the prospect of dying barren,[10] when a bright (?) idea cropped up in her mind; to use Hagar, an alien handmaid of hers, as a surrogate mother. As she put the idea to her husband, she must have been overcome by a sense of humiliation: "Please embrace her. I may be able to retrieve my reputation thanks to her" (Gn 16.2).

In the Bible we encounter quite a few women who bore the same pain and sorrow as Sarai. One such is Rachel, a wife of Jacob, a future grandson of Sarai. Because Rachel was confident that she was Jacob's favourite wife as against her elder sister Leah, to see three boys produced by Leah for Jacob must have been all the more hurting. One day, she decided to take recourse to the tactic her grandmother had adopted, about which she must have heard often. Swallowing the sense of pride, she said to Jacob: "Please embrace Bilhah, my handmaid. Then she may conceive(, place a baby) on my knees, and I, too, may retrieve my reputation thanks to her" (Gn 30.3). She must have known that there was no absolute certainty that Bilhah would become pregnant just as Hagar. Rachel must have been desperate.

These two stories must have been well known to our Septuagint translator, who also probably noted that what Sarai and Rachel each said to their respective husband looked very similar in the Hebrew original. According to the Septuagint, Sarai is supposed to have said: "Therefore, please embrace my handmaid. You will be able to make kids through her." By contrast, Rachel said, according to the Septuagint: "Please embrace her. She will then give birth (to a baby and place it) on my knees, and I also may be able to make kids through her." There is a rather subtle difference here. The Greek verb for 'make kids' is compounded of a noun meaning 'child' and a verb meaning 'to make,' and is a translation of the same Hebrew verb used in both passages. It is a very common word in the

---

[10] We have no idea whether it had ever occurred to her that her husband might be to blame. In purely medical terms such a possibility was surely there. However, in the Bible and in other ancient literatures alike, it is invariably women that are blamed. When Jacob was threatened by Rachel, who said "If you don't get me pregnant, I shall die," answered "That's God's fault" (Gn 30.1-2). He was dead right, because he had produced three kids from her rival, Leah.

sense of 'to build,' and is in the passive voice here, hence 'I can be built up,' that is, 'by bearing a child, I can make an important contribution to the future prosperity and building up of the family into which I have married.' What is striking here is that, in the former passage, the Greek verb is in the second person, making Abram the subject of the verb, whereas in the second passage the same Greek verb is in the first person, making Rachel its subject. Moreover, the form put in the mouth of Rachel is in the middle voice just as in Gn 19 with the verb for 'to wash feet' (see above at pp. 94f.). Rachel was, so to speak, saying that she was just using Bilhah as a tool for her own aim. By contrast, with the shift from the first to the second person, Sarai is concerned not so much about her own reputation as about her husband's.[11] The short word, *too*, in Rachel's "I, too" is indicative of her jealousy and rivalry, cf. Gn 30.1. This may have been noticed by our translator. Here, then, we see the translator viewing the two women in the same difficulty from two different perspectives.[12]

In the Bible there appear, in addition to Hagar and Bilhah, other women who served as surrogates. One such example is Zilpah (Gn 30.9). Of those women it is only Hagar in whom the Bible displays some interest in her subsequent life.

It was Sarai that suggested to her husband the idea of Hagar as a surrogate mother. And yet, once a baby was born, there may have been occasions when Hagar received more attention from Abram than in the past, which made Sarai feel that her standing vis-à-vis Abram was suffering, and she pestered Hagar from time to time. Hagar, on her part, couldn't stand this maltreatment by her mistress and ran away. An angel of God caught up with her in her flight and said: "Return to your mistress, and submit yourself to her maltreatment" (Gn 16.9). The Hebrew verb at vs. 6 that can be translated with 'maltreat' comes from the same root[13] as that translated with 'maltreatment' (vs. 9). However, the Septuagint reads at vs. 6 'she maltreated her,' whereas at vs. 9 it reads 'Submit yourself to subjugation to her.' The translator probably could not bring himself to writing 'Submit yourself to her maltreatment.' One could detect here his

---

[11] Another interesting detail is that, at Gn 16.3, the Hebrew original says: "Sarai, Abram's wife, brought Hagar the Egyptian, her handmaid .. and handed her to Abram her husband." The Septuagint changes 'her handmaid' to 'her own handmaid,' emphasising that this is Sarai's own initiative, not suggested by her husband.

Furthermore, "on my knees" suggests Rachel's assumption that, should a baby be born, it shall be hers, whereas Sarai, speaking to Abram, refers to Ishmael as 'her [= Hagar's] son' (Gn 21.10), though she may have wanted to oppose Ishmael to Isaac born by herself.

[12] In a case like this it is not impossible that the Hebrew text used by our translator had the verb in the second person. But no such Hebrew manuscript is known at the moment.

[13] On the notion of 'root,' see above at p. 37.

compassion towards the victim. He is doing his best to comfort and encourage her. He goes on: Don't you worry about still births, No, you will bear to your master a healthy baby, a baby boy to be followed by many more descendants, as God has promised to Abram, your master (vs. 10-12). At vs. 11 the Hebrew original says: "Jahweh heard your voice raised as you were being maltreated," for which the Septuagint reads: "the Lord tuned His ears to your voice raised as you were being subjugated."

In her ninetieth year Sarah, through God's intervention, gave birth to a baby after a long, long wait. Though born by a handmaid, Ishmael had the same rights as Isaac, as both had the same father. Sarah found this unbearable, and started pestering Hagar. One day, when Sarah saw Ishmael having fun, she exploded, urged her husband to throw both Hagar and her son out. They left, carrying hardly any chattel with them. The water container, which Abraham had given them out of compassion, was now empty, and they kept walking in the wilderness, not knowing where to. An angel of God spoke to her: "Hagar, what's the matter with you? No need to worry. God has listened to your boy's voice" (Gn 21.17). In the preceding verse, however, the Hebrew text says: "(Having cast the boy under a bush), she walked away and sat alone and over against, about the distance of a bowshot. 'I can't possibly watch him, as he dies,' she thought. She sat over against, raised her voice and wept." In the Septuagint, however, this verse concludes with ".. she sat over against him, and the child, having raised his voice, wept." It is not his mother that wept. The Greek translator may be attempting to harmonise the text with the following verse, which starts off with "God listened to the voice of the child." However, the translator's attention may have shifted from the mother to her child. He may have thought that God did not just receive sound waves, but caught the voice the child could not utter. At the opening of vs. 17 our translator uses a verb meaning 'to listen attentively, turn ears to.' The Hebrew text says that the boy's voice reached God, whereas later in the verse it says "He tuned His ears to listen to the boy's voice." This appears to have been picked up by the Greek translator, who uses two distinct verbs, though sharing the same stem, /akúo:/ 'hear.' Moreover, the first verb is in the Aorist aspect, and the second in the Perfect aspect, as if to say that the boy's weeping was still ringing in the angel's ears.[14]

Talking about the aspect in Greek, we see that, in vs. 16, the Septuagint uses two synonymous verbs for 'to sit,' for which the Hebrew text uses an identical form twice. The first Greek verb is in the Present aspect: she remained seated there. The second, however, is in the Aorist, which is the same with the following

---

[14] On the grammatical category called 'aspect,' see above at pp. 72-76.

two verbs for "lifting his voice, the child wept." The translator may have noticed a simple Hebrew preposition meaning 'to' added to the verb for 'to sit' in the first instance, focusing on Hagar's painful solitude.[15]

The Greek translator's favourable view on Sarah has been mentioned above, p. 97. When she got Abraham drive away Hagar together with her child, how did her husband react? The Hebrew text says: "the matter, i.e. Sarah's demand, was very evil according to Abraham's view" (Gn 21.11). The Septuagint, however, reads: "the matter was very difficult." The Greek adjective, /skle:rós/ 'difficult,' occurs more than 50 times in the Greek Old Testament. The range of its meanings is: 'hard to the touch; hard (of a person's character); hard to bear and mentally painful; stubborn; hard of execution.' It is never used in the sense of 'morally, ethically evil.' By contrast, the Hebrew verb used here is often so used.[16] Especially when it is combined as here with a phrase 'in the view of, according to the judgement of,' the Greek word chosen is predominantly /pone:rós/, which, in this combination, cannot be understood otherwise. Though a son born by his own wife's handmaid, Ishmael was a son of Abraham all the same. To throw him out together with his mother and deprive him of the right of inheritance was not right. To Hagar, who after having conceived, fled from her mistress, an angel of God promised a bright future. But Abraham valued his own wife's son and could not neglect her situation. He thus found himself in an impossible conundrum. Then God offered him a helping hand: "As far as that boy and your handmaid are concerned, listen to everything that Sarah says. Your posterity will be named after Isaac. But I shall make the son of the handmaid a great nation, for you have begotten him" (vs. 12-13). God was confronted with a difficult problem. Here, too, the Greek translator seems to be refraining from making a bad woman of Sarah.

An example in which the idiomatic Hebrew phrase at the beginning of vs. 11 is devoid of any ethical nuance is found at Gn 48.17. It is a scene in which, Jacob, sensing that his earthly life is fast drawing to an end, blessed two sons of his beloved son, Joseph. With his eyesight failing, he wrongly places his hand on Ephraim, a younger grandson. Thinking that the blessing was due to Manasseh, the first-born, Joseph intervened. The Septuagint has here: "this came over to him [= Joseph] as unbearable."

An interesting example occurs in the book of Jonah, which was most likely translated by another person. The Hebrew expression concerned, though not

---

[15] On this nuance of the Hebrew preposition, see above on Gn 22.2, p. 27.

[16] We have mentioned above (pp. 41f.) an instance in which David used this Hebrew expression devoid of moral dimension.

identical word for word with that we have been looking at in Genesis, is very similar none the less. When Jonah saw the mass repentance of Ninevites, starting with the king down to domestic animals, "Jonah was rather displeased and became angry," so in Hebrew at Jon 4.1. The Septuagint, however, reads: "Jonah was very much grieved and confused." He was not very happy to make a long journey to Nineveh in the first place and thought that wicked Ninevites had better be punished by God and die off. This unexpected turn of events, however, meant in his view that his arduous journey was for nothing, and he was absolutely dissatisfied. His displeasure was not directed at Ninevites, but at God Himself. The Greek translator of the Twelve Prophets may not have been comfortable with the idea of a human being getting angry at God.

Coming back to the story of Hagar, we read at Gn 21.19: "God opened her eyes, and she saw a well of water. She went there, filled the skin with water, and gave the child to drink." For "a well of water" the Septuagint reads "a well of living water." Living water refers to fresh water gushing out of a well or fountain, not 'lifeless' water in a pool. At Gn 26.19 the Hebrew original also reads a phrase which would correspond to what we read in the Septuagint at 21.19. We do not know whether or not the Hebrew text used by the translator differed[17] from the traditional text. If not, why did he add this extra word meaning 'life'? The water shown by God to Hagar became literally 'water of life' for the boy fast dying from dehydration. The living water, of which Jesus spoke to the Samaritan woman (Joh 4.10), is the same in Greek as in the Septuagint of Gn 21.19.

The wilderness of Beersheba, where Hagar and her son wandered, was arid and dry. Their ancestors had their eyes opened at the tree of life in the lush, verdant Garden of Eden, ushering in death as our destiny. Here God Himself opened Hagar's eyes in the direction of the water securing life. As he worked on Gn 21, our translator may have remembered Gn 2 and 3 he had translated earlier.

E) The Septuagint in relation to the New Testament

At this point we move to a closer look at the relationship between the Septuagint and the New Testament.

It is generally thought that, unlike the Apostle Paul, Luke the fourth Evangelist was not very knowledgeable about Hebrew and Aramaic. On the other hand, there are indications that he was well versed in the Greek Old Testament. At the end of

---

[17] No such Hebrew manuscript of the Bible is known at the moment.

the Gospel we meet two despondent believers walking to Emmaus in the suburbs of Jerusalem, and they are met by resurrected Jesus. Initially their eyes were held back from recognising Him (Lk 24.16). As He walked on alongside them, He explained to them from the Prophets how the Messiah they were looking forward to was described. When they entered an inn and sat at the table, He took bread, blessed it, broke it, and began to hand it to them, then all of a sudden their eyes were opened and they recognised Him (vs. 31). They probably had heard of what had happened at the Last Supper. The Greek for "their eyes opened" is the same as at the above-mentioned Gn 3.7 in the Septuagint. In the Garden of Even, death ensued when the first human couple's eyes opened. The two on the way to Emmaus, when their eyes opened, they met the One who had triumphed over death and would give us eternal life.

Of the four Gospel writers Luke alone has preserved the parable of the prodigal son. He describes in detail how the father, who had been waiting for his son's return home day and night, reacted one day when he spotted his dear son still at quite a distance: "he was still far off, but on spying him, the father felt his intestines beginning to split into pieces, ran out, fell on his neck, and kissed him hard" (Lk 15.20). Some time ago, as I read this passage in Greek, I noticed that the three verbs used here are virtually identical with those used in Gn 33.3-4 in the Septuagint. It is in a description of Jacob, who, having parted with Laban his uncle, made a dramatic reunion with his elder brother Esau, from whose anger and bitterness Jacob had sought refuge for twenty long years: "before approaching his elder brother, he greeted, prostrating himself seven times. To welcome him, Esau ran to him, embraced him, kissed him, fell on his neck and the two wept." As he penned in Greek this moving parable told by Jesus, Luke was probably deeply conscious of this story in Genesis, which he may have known by heart. It is not just the similarity in vocabulary used in the two stories, but both are about reconciliation. Moreover, in both stories the victim runs to the perpetrator. The prodigal son decided to return home, having realised that he had sinned against his heavenly Father and his father on the earth alike. In this parable Luke may have recognised the merciful God sending His son to the world.[18]

---

[18] One scholar believes that Luke's description may also have been influenced by the story of reunion between Joseph and his brothers: "he [= Joseph] fell on the neck of Benjamin his brother and wept, with his face on it [= Benjamin's neck], and Benjamin wept with his face on his [= Joseph's] neck. Having kissed his brothers hard, he wept, holding them, and after that his brothers spoke with him" (Gn 45.14-15). True, there are some words common to the parable, and here also we have a story of reconciliation. But there are some significant differences. Joseph did

Let's look at two more examples from Luke.

In the description of the birth of the future John the Baptist to Elizabeth we read: "when her neighbours and relatives heard that the Lord had granted great mercy to her, they rejoiced with her" (Lk 1.58). The Greek verb meaning "to rejoice with (someone else)" occurs in "Sarah said: 'the Lord has made me laugh. Whoever hears (of this) would rejoice with me'" (Gn 21.6). The verb concerned is compounded of a common verb meaning 'to rejoice' and a prefix in the sense of 'together,' and occurs merely twice in the Septuagint, and is rather rarely used in the general Greek literature as well. Hence the possibility of this Septuagint passage influencing Luke is highly probable. Here again we are not talking about the vocabulary alone. The two stories have a common theme. In both stories an aged lady who had never given birth to a child became pregnant through God's direct intervention, which would lead to a dramatic development in their respective life thereafter. The two babies born were each destined to play a vital role in God's plan for the salvation of mankind.

The Hebrew words translated at Gn 21.6 'laugh' and 'rejoice' into Greek come from the same root. There is an element of ambiguity here, so that some scholars go as far as to suggest that this is about derisive, scornful laugh. Our Greek translator, however, translating the second instance with 'to rejoice together' is obviously looking at a positive, bright side, and must have interpreted the first instance in a similar fashion. Neighbours of Sarah, who had been pitied as a poor barren old wife, heard now, passing by her tent, a chuckling old mother fondling Isaac.

The last example from Luke concerns the virtue of humility Jesus taught a few times. Its typical example is a parable He taught, mentioning a Pharisee and a tax collector who went to the Jerusalem temple, by chance at the same time: "[9]He told the following parable about those who are confident that they are righteous and belittle others .. [14]This man [= tax collector] went home, considered (by God) righteous .. Whoever exalts himself will be brought down, and whoever humbles himself will be exalted" (Lk 18.9, 14). As he wrote this story, Luke may have been thinking of Ps 50.19, where the Septuagint reads: "A sacrifice (acceptable) to God is a broken spirit. A broken and humbled heart will God not belittle." The Hebrew original is slightly different: "Sacrifices (acceptable) to God are a broken spirit. A broken, contrite heart, o God, You will not belittle." God did not belittle the tax collector the Pharisee belittled, but rather God thought highly of the tax collector.

---

not run out to meet his brothers. Though not for the sake of reconciliation, it was the brothers that had come to Joseph. Both Esau and the father of the prodigal son acted promptly the moment they knew the identity of the other party, but it took quite a while before Joseph made his move, though he had recognised his brothers immediately on his first encounter with them.

We now turn to St Paul in relation to the Septuagint.

The most important message in Paul's teaching is justification by faith. In other words, we humans can be regarded by God as righteous not by our own merits, whatever good deeds we may do, but only when we believe in God and accept that His only son, Jesus Christ, died on the cross a death that was due to us as the price for our sinful life. Paul expresses this message as "the righteous shall live by faith" (Rom 1.17, Gal 3.11). In the former passage, Paul is quoting from the Old Testament, as we can see from his addition: "as is written." This source text is Hab 2.4, where the Hebrew original says: "the righteous shall live by his faith." This pronoun, *his*, here refers to the righteous. The Septuagint, however, reads: "my faith." This difference between the two pronouns is most likely due to the graphic ambiguity of the two Hebrew letters, which are both written as a single stroke: if written as a short stroke above, it means "my," whereas if it is vertically extended downwards, it means "his." In actual manuscripts, however, this graphic difference is not that clearcut, and the Hebrew manuscript used by the Greek translator may have been vague or he may have misread the letter. In neither of the passages mentioned above the noun *faith* has a possessive pronoun attached to it in the Septuagint. Born in Tarsus in Eastern Turkey, Paul was probably educated in Greek, in which he must have been fluent. Later, when he came to the Holy Land, he received the traditional Jewish education under Rabbi Gamaliel, and his grasp of Hebrew and Aramaic must have improved considerably. Since there was no iPad or iPhone around yet, people who were familiar with the Bible must have known quite a lot by heart. Nor was there a printed Bible available, a huge volume. Only the rich could afford a copy. Even if one had a copy, it would add to the weight of one's baggage. We can hardly think of Paul taking a copy of the entire Septuagint on his missionary travels. He was presumably capable of making his own Greek translation of verses he knew by heart in Hebrew or Aramaic.

The verb 'to live' is used here not in the sense of 'to lead a life,' but as an antonym of 'death, to die,' which we can conclude from what precedes the citation from Hab 2.4: "for I am not ashamed of the gospel, for it is God's power for everyone who believes, first for a Jew and then a Greek. God's righteousness becomes apparent in him from belief to belief, as it is written etc." (Ro 1.16-17a). For Paul, who is contrasting faith and salvation, the presence or absence of the possessive personal pronoun mattered little.

In the context *my* in "my faith" can only refer to God. The first half of vs. 4 in the Hebrew original is difficult of interpretation: "his inner soul is puffed up and not honest" is one possible understanding. By contrast, the Septuagint reads: "if he flinches (before it out of fear), My soul would not be pleased with him." Here again, as against "*my* soul" of the Septuagint, the Hebrew text reads "*his* soul," which must refer to the soul of the righteous.

In the Epistle to the Hebrews the Habakkuk passage is quoted in a slightly different form: "My righteous shall live by faith. But if he flinches, My soul would not be pleased with him" (Heb 10.38). Readers of the epistle are exhorted to remember that, when they experience persecution or hardship because of their belief in God, they should not doubt that the time of ultimate triumph will come.

Whether one prefers 'my righteous' or just 'the righteous,' one should not think that we are by nature either righteous or unrighteous. It is rather that those who choose the way of faith in God are treated by God as righteous and saved.[19]

Regarding the doctrine of justification by faith there is another Old Testament passage which meant very much to St Paul: "and he believed Jahweh and He reckoned it for him as (equivalent to) righteousness" (Gn 15.6). The Septuagint reads: "and Abram believed God, and it was reckoned for him as (equivalent) to righteousness," which is completely identical with Ro 4.3. The same appears with very minor variations in Ro 4.9 and Gal 3.6. What is striking here is the shift from the active (Hebrew in Gn 15.6) to passive (Septuagint there). In terms of the general import the formulation in the two voices amounts to no significant difference.[20]

Is Paul quoting at Ro 4.3 from Gn 15.6 in its Septuagint formulation or providing a Greek translation made up by him from the Hebrew text, where the verb in question can only be viewed as being in the active voice? One Dead Sea

---

[19] Among the Dead Sea scrolls there is found a commentary written in Hebrew on the book of Habakkuk. Unfortunately, in this partly fragmentary document, the text of Hab 2.4b has not been preserved, so that we do not know which pronoun was attached to it. The comments which follow, however, are well preserved: "This refers to all who practise the law in the house of Judah, whom God will rescue out of the court on account of their endeavour and faith in the teacher of righteousness" (1QpHab 8.1-3). There is no evidence of direct contact between this Qumran community on the one hand and St Paul and the early church on the other. In any event the teaching represented in this document is diametrically opposed to Paul's theological position.

[20] The Septuagint sentence in the passive voice at Gn 15.6 recurs in the exactly same form in Ps 106.31 in Hebrew, and its Septuagint reading is 100% identical with Gn 15.6. We would only note that, in this Ps passage, what was reckoned as equivalent to righteousness is the mediation between God and his people undertaken by Phinehas, and not his faith. In Ps 106.31 the Hebrew verb in question is manifestly in the passive voice.

At both Gn 15.6 and Ro 4.3 there is no substantive in the context that might be being referred to with the pronoun *it*. In the Hebrew text at Gn 15.6, however, it is a feminine pronoun, which may reflect a substantive meaning 'faith,' a substantive which is feminine in gender. In Ro 4.9 there is no place for doubt as Paul writes: "The faith was reckoned for Abraham as (equivalent) to righteousness." In Ps 106.31, too, the verb is feminine with no feminine substantive in the context. The psalmist may be thinking of the zeal displayed by Phinehas (Nu 25.11); the noun for *zeal* is of feminine gender.

document throws an interesting light on this question. The text is the book of Jubilees, also known as mini-Genesis, a document generally thought to date from the second half of the second century BCE. This belongs to what is known as pseudepigrapha. Until a few Hebrew fragments of this document were identified among the Qumran documents, it was known in its entirety in an Ethiopic translation made from its Greek version. In a passage which corresponds to Gn 15.6 one of the Qumran Hebrew fragments reads exactly as in the Septuagint. The verb in question is in the passive voice. Though this text was written slightly later than the Septuagint of the book of Genesis, it is rather unlikely that the author of *Jubilees* translated the Septuagint into Hebrew. Paul, then, was not necessarily and deliberately quoting Gn 15.6 from its Septuagint version, but knew a contemporary, Jewish interpretation of Gn 15.6. The Septuagint may also reflect at Gn 15.6 such a contemporary, scholarly milieu.

At Gn 15.6 both the Hebrew verb translated with 'believed' and its Greek translation mean 'trusted.' Abram, though promised by God a bright, prosperous future, had no child at the age of 90, and started questioning what God really meant. When, however, he was taken outdoors and told to look above and heard God say "Look at the stars in the sky. Your descendants will be as many. Nothing is impossible with God," he *believed*, i.e. decided to trust God. This is quite clear in Paul's further elaboration on the subject of justification by faith. When God told Abram that He would make him a father of nations (Gn 17.4), he must have believed against belief, namely, he decided to trust God, though, humanly speaking, God's promise sounded unbelievable (Ro 4.16-18). We may think that our sinful condition is hopeless and death alone is our destiny, but Jesus willingly and mercifully died on the cross to pay our penalty of death, and rose again from the dead, having defeated death. By accepting this Gospel message without doubting, we could be saved. This is Paul's message. Hymns "Jesus, my Lord, to thee I cry" (Eliza H. Hamilton) and "Amazing grace" (John Newton) come to one's mind.

In Conclusion

I am not sure to what extent I have succeeded in convincing you that, by reading the Bible in its original languages, you can at times understand its meaning and message better or differently than reading it in a modern translation. I have done my best to share with you what I have learned by reading the Bible in its original languages and its ancient translations over some sixty years.

I know very well that Hebrew, Aramaic, and Greek are distinct in sounds, grammar, and vocabulary from many other languages, one of which may be your mother tongue. One consolation for native speakers of Chinese and Japanese is that Hebrew and Aramaic are written with only twenty-two letters and Greek with twenty-four.

There are many beginners' grammars to the biblical languages available in many languages on the market. There are also bilingual dictionaries for them. I have also recently added my own: *A Biblical Aramaic Reader with an Outline Grammar*, 83 pages (Peeters: Leuven, 2015) and *A Biblical Hebrew Reader with an Outline Grammar*, 139 pages (Peeters: Leuven, 2017).

It is my sincere hope that these biblical languages are kept being taught and researched at theological seminaries and divinity schools throughout the world, including Asia.

I conclude by expressing my sense of gratitude to Peeters Publishing in Leuven for agreeing to publish this book and to Mr Bert Verrept and his staff there for taking good care of its production. Keiko, my wife, also read the draft through in its Japanese version and offered useful comments.

Takamitsu MURAOKA
Professor emeritus
Leiden University
The Netherlands.

25 May 2019

INDICES

A) Biblical texts[1]

[1] Where long biblical passages are discussed verse after verse, no page reference is given here to those verses.

	15.20	101			9.36	81
	18.9, 14	102			16.28	50
	24.6	75		Ro	1.16-17a	103
	24.16, 31	101			1.17	103
Joh	1.42	81			4.3	104
	4.10	100			4.9	104
	6.48	70			4.16-18	105
	8.32	71			8.15	81
	10.11	70			13.8	89
	11.24	53		1Cor	10.13	26
	12.3	74			15.3-5	75
	13.1	74			16.22	81
	13.14	89		Gal	3.6	104
	14.6	70, 71			3.11	103
	15.12, 17	89, 90		Eph	5.25	90
	15.13, 14, 15	90, 92		1Tim	2.15	96
	18.38	71		Heb	10.38	104
	21.15-17	91			11.1, 17, 19	29
Acts	1.19	81		Jam	1.2	26
	9.1-6	75			1.13	26

B) Hebrew, Aramaic, and Greek words

a) Hebrew[2]

aháv	אָהַב	91
el	אֵל	82
elóah	אֱלֹהַ	82
et	אֵת	27
bará	בָּרָא	89
yosef	יוֹסֵף	34
mélekh tov	מֶלֶךְ טוֹב	81
qaná	קָנָה	89
ra	רַע	41
shakháv	שָׁכַב	65

b) Aramaic

abbá	אַבָּא	81
chaqél dmá	חֲקֵל דְּמָא	81
tbithá	טְבִיתָא	81
tlitá qum	טְלִיתָא קוּמִי	81

yáyin	יַיִן	84
kefa	כֵּיפָא	81
mélekh tav	מֶלֶךְ טָב	81
marána thá	מָרַנָא תָא	81
shvaqtáni	שְׁבַקְתַּנִי	81

c) Greek

agapáo:	ἀγαπάω	89, 90, 91
agápe:	ἀγάπη	89, 90, 92
eráo:	ἐράω	89
éro:s	ἔρως	89
ké:rygma	κήρυγμα	75
óinos	οἶνος	84
splangkh-nízomai	σπλαγχνίζομαι	71
filéo:	φιλέω	89, 91
filía:	φιλία	89
fílos	φίλος	90, 92

---

[2] For Hebrew and Aramaic words approximative pronunciation is shown in the first column. Their forms are sometimes slightly different from how they appear in the Greek New Testament.

PRINTED ON PERMANENT PAPER • IMPRIME SUR PAPIER PERMANENT • GEDRUKT OP DUURZAAM PAPIER - ISO 9706

N.V. PEETERS S.A., WAROTSTRAAT 50, B-3020 HERENT